"Most school data attest what has happened and what students can and cannot do, and thus looks backward. COVID-19-era teaching has amplified the value of seeking evidence to also look forward. Data needs to help us make decisions about the next best teaching and learning steps and be bold yet confident in making predictions of future learning. Stepan Mekhitarian invites us to be bold, look forward, learn from our experiences during COVID-19, harness technology, and accelerate learning."

"'Formative assessment' is not about assessment. Instead, it is a teaching philosophy that uses evidence (from tests, student work, student voice about their progress, and teacher observation) to optimally make judgments about the next best teaching and learning steps. This message is evident in every chapter of these two complementary books—for teachers and leaders—which makes Dr. Mekhitarian's message so powerful. Worthwhile data must lead to actions, acceleration, advancing confidence, and advising about impact for leaders, teachers, and students."

—**John Hattie,** Emeritus Laureate Professor in the Graduate School of Education at the University of Melbourne

"Timely, relevant, and immediately applicable, these companion books by Dr. Mekhitarian offer just-in-time, responsive strategies for both teachers and school leaders interested in using formative assessment data to support students' learning in today's rapidly changing education landscape."

—**Kasia Faughn,** Assessment Communication Program Manager, Sacramento County Office of Education

"Dr. Stepan Mekhitarian provides a timely resource for public schools to reimagine their student-data practices. These companion books succinctly address the climate in which we are educating and how to improve instruction despite recent gaps in performance data. Leveraging the speed and accuracy of technology to transform formative assessment practices is how we, as educators, accelerate learning and dig ourselves out of learning loss caused by the pandemic."

—**Robyn Anders,** Coordinator of Instructional Technology, Burbank Unified School District

"Dr. Mekhitarian is a sought-after subject matter expert in the state of California who shares his vast knowledge of the formative assessment process in a way that is both robust and easy for readers to understand. These fantastic companion books include space to reflect on thought-provoking prompts that help us engage in the learning in a deeper and more meaningful way, and the tips called out throughout the books are pure gold!"

—**Nikki Antonovich,** Coordinator, Center for Student Assessment and Program Accountability, Sacramento County Office of Education

"Dr. Mekhitarian gives teachers and school leaders the tools necessary to help all students in the twenty-first-century blended classroom. He invites educators to reflect on student learning, involves us in the analysis of data collection, and offers real and meaningful direction in the pursuit of maximizing the effectiveness of formative data. This book is a great guide for any educator looking to leverage the power of formative data to innovate learning."

—**Matthieu Hamo,** Sixth Grade Teacher, Glendale Unified School District

"Dr. Mekhitarian is a seasoned educational leader who tirelessly continues his firm commitment to instructional innovations and academic excellence. His companion books are essential for any educator interested in using formative data to make great decisions for students. They are practical, informative, effective, inspiring, and timely, especially as we come out of the pandemic and reflect on what's next in education. The companion books are undoubtedly must-have resources for professional development in schools, districts, and teacher preparation programs."

—**Silva S. Karayan,** Professor Emeritus of Education, California Lutheran University

"Stepan's innovative approach on formative assessment in a virtual setting has had a vast impact on our academy. The way he dives deep into the purpose and importance of meaningful checks for understanding has changed the way our teachers create, implement, and analyze assessments."

—**Erika Tumminelli,** Principal, Salinas City Virtual Academy

"Dr. Mekhitarian's two new companion books make the cogent case that formative assessments are not just checks for understanding, but key tools in fostering systemic and organizational change for the benefit of all students. By following the suggested activities, teachers and administrators can begin to dialogue about the role of formative assessments with respect to their schools' mission and vision, and figure out how to maximize the impact of these tools given a changing educational landscape spurred on by the pandemic and recent technological advances."

—**Paul Hsu,** Director and Co-Founder, Lotus Creek Foundation and t space Taiwan

"Dr. Mekhitarian provides a comprehensive, step-by-step process to help teachers and school leaders make formative data the primary driver in decision-making. His books offer key insights as to how schools can build a sense of shared accountability and urgency to meet the needs of all students. As a school district leader, Dr. Mekhitarian knows firsthand the challenges of building a strong data culture. His recommendations are practical and actionable, featuring timely advice on leveraging technology and empowering teachers and administrators to use formative data to promote equity in schools."

—**Evan Bartelheim,** Project Director,
Accountability & Data Literacy,
Los Angeles County Office of Education

"Finding the balance between gathering data to inform our instruction and respecting our classroom instructional time is a battle that teachers invariably struggle with. Dr. Mekhitarian's book takes us through both the theory and the practicality of achieving that balance. He shows educators how accessing and sharing data, using the technological tools that are available to everyone today, can make a beneficial difference in our teaching and in our students' learning.

—**Shannon M. Clark-Reed,** English Teacher and Instructional Technology Coach, Glendale Unified School District

"The principle that grounds my work is that all students deserve to thrive in an inclusive environment supported by adults who put them at the center of every conversation. Dr. Mekhitarian's innovative approach to post-pandemic formative assessment provides an actionable plan to guide school/student/teaching improvement efforts."

—**Vivian Ekchian,** Superintendent,
Glendale Unified School District

As education evolves from the adjustments made for distance learning, Dr. Mekhitarian's timely book provides actionable steps for teachers to use newly learned instructional technologies to implement formative assessments that provide real-time feedback for students and teachers. From beginning to end of the text, I felt empowered to implement meaningful formative assessments that bring equity and differentiation to my classroom.

—**Michelle Manalo,** Elementary Teacher,
John Muir Elementary School

"Dr. Mekhitarian's companion books are texts that provide educators with the tools they need in order to outline how to best utilize data. These texts allow readers to carve out their paths towards data analysis and establish best practices for utilizing the data to support learning. I have worked with Dr. Mekhitarian on many occasions to create systems to best incorporate the ideas suggested in his books. We have been successful in our results and continue to further develop and incorporate his strategies. I highly recommend these texts."
—**Mary Mardirosian,** Assistant Principal, Herbert Hoover High School

"These books are a staple that need to be in the hands of every instructional leader and classroom teacher. Dr. Stepan Mekhitarian provides valuable insight on how to effectively utilize formative data to improve student learning. Moreover, he addresses how to foster a data-driven culture, providing actionable steps that will help every school site reach its full potential."
—**Natalie Kontogiannis,** Director of Curriculum, Instruction, and Innovation, AGBU Manoogian-Demirdjian School

"The development of technology has delivered more data to schools than ever before. In these two companion volumes, Dr. Mekhitarian lays out a roadmap for teachers and administrators to leverage the data schools collect into timely actions for both the larger organization and the classroom. This work provides the connection between the data-rich world of high-stakes school evaluation and the inside-the-classroom moves made by each teacher. Using side-by-side texts focused on simple moves for the teacher and school leader with supportive and practical implementation tips, Dr. Mekhitarian's work will allow your school to develop a vision around what educators can learn from the use of formative data and how it will positively impact schools, teachers, and students."

—**Elias Miles,** Assistant Superintendent, Fillmore Unified School District

"In a time when many educators are struggling to address the current challenges, Stepan brings his expertise and authenticity to provide support in this space. These two companion books provide practical steps to infuse formative assessment with educational technology to foster a growth mindset and increase student learning. Stepan effectively communicates both a vision and practical steps to operationalize this vision. These books are accessible for teachers and organizational leaders with a focus on increasing student agency and success."

—**Dave Chun,** Director, Mathematics, Sacramento County Office of Education

"Though most educators say they recognize the critical nature of formative assessment (FA), observations demonstrate repeatedly that teachers simply do not collect or utilize real-time data as often or as well as they should. Mekhitarian's practical text not only clarifies the 'what' of FA but, more importantly, lays out the 'how' in a way that is extremely doable for busy teachers. His connections to technology, differentiation, social justice, and research throughout the text help to emphasize the importance, rationale, and ease of using regular, well-crafted FA in the K-12 classroom. The inclusion of questions, prompts, templates, tables, and key takeaways offers a scaffolding for readers as they consider their own situations and determine how to embed more formative data collection in their own practice."

—**Wendy Murawski, PhD,** Eisner Endowed Chair & Executive Director, Center for Teaching & Learning, California State University Northridge

"Dr. Mekhitarian compels us to consider our own beliefs about student learning and the role we play in making meaning out of rich, daily interactions with students within our classrooms. This book is not a primer but rather a solution-focused journey for practitioners who wish to promote equity through formative practices and use real-time data to make informed decisions about our teaching and their learning."

—**Jessica Conkle,** Director 1, Los Angeles County Office of Education

"These two books provide school leaders and teachers with a wealth of knowledge and practical applications for implementing formative assessment practices and using data in real time to inform both classroom instruction and professional learning. These books are particularly timely in the context of the transition back to classroom-based instruction from time spent in distance or hybrid learning experiences. Educators are immersed in a changing landscape brought on not only by pandemic-based impacts on learning contexts but also by challenging academic standards and ever-evolving real-world contexts into which our students will become future workers and citizens. These books can support educational leaders and classroom educators to select high-quality assessment strategies, collect immediately actionable data to feed back into teaching and learning, and apply both the assessment practices and the data to promote social justice and ensure equity and access to rigorous learning and academic outcomes."

—**Sally J. Bennett-Schmidt,** Retired Director of Assessment, San Diego County Office of Education

Harnessing Formative Data for K-12 Teachers

Harnessing Formative Data for K-12 Teachers prepares teachers to apply real-time formative data to classroom instruction amid the expansion of online and blended learning in schools. In today's changing, technology-enhanced educational landscape, teachers must rethink how to generate and use formative data to inform planning and develop systems that lead to *all* students' success. This book's strategic insights into actionable formative data use will yield differentiated supports for students, helping teachers to foster greater academic outcomes, independent self-monitoring, and readiness for college, career, and lifelong learning. Each chapter includes connections to social justice, best practices for applying data points and field-tested tips for technology integration, and a host of interactive planning guides to support implementation.

Stepan Mekhitarian is Director of Innovation, Instruction, Assessment & Accountability at Glendale Unified School District in California.

Also Available from Routledge
Eye On Education
(www.routledge.com/k-12)

Teaching as Protest
Emancipating Classrooms Through Racial Consciousness
Robert S. Harvey and Susan Gonzowitz

The Brain-Based Classroom
Accessing Every Child's Potential Through Educational Neuroscience
Kieran O'Mahony

Thriving as an Online K-12 Educator
Essential Practices from the Field
Edited by Jody Peerless Green

The Media-Savvy Middle School Classroom
Strategies for Teaching Against Disinformation
Susan Brooks-Young

Five Teaching and Learning Myths—Debunked
A Guide for Teachers
Adam M. Brown and Althea Need Kaminske

Differentiated Instruction Made Practical
Engaging the Extremes through Classroom Routines
Rhonda Bondie and Akane Zusho

Harnessing Formative Data for K-12 Teachers

Real-time Classroom Strategies

Stepan Mekhitarian

Routledge
Taylor & Francis Group
NEW YORK AND LONDON

Cover image: Shutterstock

First published 2023
by Routledge
605 Third Avenue, New York, NY 10158

and by Routledge
4 Park Square, Milton Park, Abingdon, Oxon, OX14 4RN

Routledge is an imprint of the Taylor & Francis Group, an informa business

© 2023 Stepan Mekhitarian

The right of Stepan Mekhitarian to be identified as author of this work has been asserted in accordance with sections 77 and 78 of the Copyright, Designs and Patents Act 1988.

All rights reserved. No part of this book may be reprinted or reproduced or utilised in any form or by any electronic, mechanical, or other means, now known or hereafter invented, including photocopying and recording, or in any information storage or retrieval system, without permission in writing from the publishers.

Trademark notice: Product or corporate names may be trademarks or registered trademarks, and are used only for identification and explanation without intent to infringe.

Library of Congress Cataloging-in-Publication Data
Names: Mekhitarian, Stepan, author.
Title: Harnessing formative data for K-12 teachers : real-time classroom strategies / Stepan Mekhitarian.
Description: New York, NY : Routledge, 2023. | Includes bibliographical references and index.
Identifiers: LCCN 2022019943 (print) | LCCN 2022019944 (ebook) | ISBN 9781032158051 (hardback) | ISBN 9781032159027 (paperback) | ISBN 9781003246213 (ebook)
Subjects: LCSH: Education—Data processing. | Academic achievement. | Curriculum planning. | Effective teaching.
Classification: LCC LB1028.43 .M45 2023 (print) | LCC LB1028.43 (ebook) | DDC 371.33/4—dc23/eng/20220701
LC record available at https://lccn.loc.gov/2022019943
LC ebook record available at https://lccn.loc.gov/2022019944

ISBN: 978-1-032-15805-1 (hbk)
ISBN: 978-1-032-15902-7 (pbk)
ISBN: 978-1-003-24621-3 (ebk)

DOI: 10.4324/9781003246213

Typeset in Palatino
by Apex CoVantage, LLC

Contents

Foreword xvii
Preface xix
Acknowledgments xxiii
About the Author xxv

PART I
**The Need to Reevaluate How We Use Data
in the Classroom** 1

**Introduction: Changing Instructional Data
Considerations** 3
- Advancements in Technology Changing
  Formative Data Use 6
  - Instructional Technology Creates New
    Opportunities to Gather and Use Data 8
  - Identifying *Actionable* Data From a Sea
    of Data Points 11
- Loss of Consistent Summative Data From
  Previous Academic Years 13
  - Continuity of Data Points Disrupted by
    Changing Events 14
  - Continuity of Data Points Disrupted by
    Changing Standards 14
- Concerns About Data Reliability Due to
  Increased Remote Assessment 15
- Concerns About "Learning Loss" During
  Distance Learning 16
- Key Takeaways 17

1 Your Classroom's Vision and Beliefs 19
- Assessing Your Classroom Vision..................... 20
- Reflecting on Your Beliefs About Student Learning and Your Role 26
- Where Formative Data Fits In 29
- Key Takeaways 33

2 The Impact of Formative Data on Student Success 35
- Formative Data Fosters Students' Growth Mindset 36
- Formative Data Informs Instruction................... 39
- Formative Data Facilitates Differentiation and Promotes Equity 42
- Key Takeaways 47

PART II
Effective Formative Data Use in the New Classroom 49

3 Maximizing the Effectiveness of Formative Data 51
- How *Actionable* Is the Data You Are Gathering?........ 54
  - Actionable Data Is Easily Accessible 55
  - Actionable Data Can Be Understood by Students 57
  - Actionable Data Utilizes Instructional Technology to Maximize Differentiation............ 62
- How *Timely* Is the Data You Are Gathering?........... 64
  - How Soon Will You Be Able to Act On the Data?....................................... 65
- How Much Data Do You Need? 67
  - How Much Time Will It Take to Collect the Data, and Will You Be Able to Address All the Data You Collect? 68
- Key Takeaways 68

4 Using Instructional Technology to Effectively Address Formative Data ... 69
- On-the-Fly Formative Data for Whole Class Instruction ... 71
  - Polling ... 73
  - Keyword Programs ... 74
  - Quick Surveys ... 74
- Formative Assessments for Differentiated Learning ... 75
  - Common Formative Assessments Generated Through Instructional Technology ... 75
  - Formative Assessments Built Into Lesson Presentations ... 79
  - Checks for Understanding to Inform Small Group Instruction ... 80
  - Gathering Formative Data Through Different Learning Modalities ... 81
  - Student-Generated Formative Assessments ... 83
- Key Takeaways ... 84

5 Building Student Capacity Through Formative Data ... 87
- Digital Self-Assessment Rubrics ... 90
- Self-Selected Small Groups ... 94
- Self-Monitored Digital Success Trackers ... 97
- Key Takeaways ... 99

6 Analyzing Formative Data Collaboratively to Identify and Celebrate Best Practices ... 101
- PLCs ... 103
- Peer Observations—In-Person and Virtual ... 105
- Teacher-Led Professional Development ... 107
- Success Celebration Events ... 109
- Key Takeaways ... 111

7 Innovative Learning in the New Classroom 113
- Re-envisioning Learning for All Students............116
- Reflecting on the Focus on Summative and Formative Assessments 120
- Preparing Students to Be Lifelong Independent Learners 121
- Key Takeaways 122

Conclusion 123
References 125
Index 129

Foreword

When we published *Blended Learning in Action*, we aimed to provide leaders and teachers with a practical resource to support the integration of technology in classrooms through the models codified and published by the Christensen Institute. However, the outcome toward which we were driving was not the use of technology itself. Rather, the big "why" driving blended learning was to better serve every student by making learning more personalized and student-centered. To ensure a focus on this outcome over technology use alone, we introduced the hallmarks of effective blended learning—personalization, student agency, authenticity, connectivity, and creativity—all of which are supported by the formative data that teachers would be able to better access through digital tools and curriculum.

When we met Stepan, it was immediately clear that he was a blended learning champion and trailblazer focused on that shared destination. In his district leadership role, he uses the strategies shared in *Blended Learning in Action* to help teachers tap into new learning data using technology to empower students as agents of their learning. As we founded our company LINC, the Learning Innovation Catalyst, we wanted to bring personalized professional learning to teachers so they could experience the type of learning they were striving to create in their classrooms. We began collaborating with Stepan to create professional development resources and easy-to-use learning activities, which became some of the foundational tools for our company's first clients. Stepan's work as an early author of LINCspring content has reached thousands of teachers.

In *Harnessing Formative Data for K-12 Teachers*, Stepan created a work to deepen educator practice in data-informed learning design and instruction. He pairs these strategies with those focused on building student capacity and agency to reflect upon their own learning progress, set new goals, and attain them. In LINC's research Model of Generative Change, by Dr. Arnetha Ball, we call this essential mindset and learning cycle "generativity." This book, along with its companion work, *Harnessing Formative Data for K-12 Leaders*, provides leaders and teachers with the timely and actionable guides they need to put generativity at the forefront of learning to enable every student to succeed.

Tiffany Wycoff and Jason Green,
Co-authors of *Blended Learning in Action*

Preface

The changing educational landscape brought about by the transition to distance learning means educators must rethink how to generate and use formative data. After an unexpected distance learning experience with limited summative data access, we are in a unique position to pause and reset our thinking on data and its role in instructional planning. This is an unprecedented opportunity to advance personalized learning through formative data with our newfound expertise with technology.

This book is designed to prepare teachers to reevaluate how they use formative data to inform instruction, planning, interventions, supports, and learning initiatives. After analyzing the benefits of formative data to student success, we will explore current challenges, such as limited actionable data points from prior years, concerns about data reliability during distance learning, and a saturation of data points created from the increased use of technology. We will then review how technology can be harnessed to address these challenges by prioritizing timely, actionable formative data, collaboratively analyzing the data and identifying best practices, and building capacity through data-driven self-monitoring. Using actionable formative data to drive planning will lead targeted and differentiated supports that result in greater student outcomes and equity to ensure all students succeed and become lifelong learners.

The flowchart presented highlights the journey through the book, including how each chapter informs the subsequent one to create a clear path from vision to implementation.

The book is designed as a companion to *Harnessing Formative Data for K-12 Leaders*, which focuses on leadership with formative data at the organizational level. These books are timely as schools and districts across the country transition back to on-campus learning and face a new reality regarding formative data. Effective use of formative data has always been a quality of high-performing educators, but its importance has been heightened since the transition to distance learning, which impacted the consistency, accuracy, availability, and actionability of data points teachers and leaders rely on to make decisions to support student learning and equity. With limited past data points and increased proficiency and experience with instructional technology during distance learning, educators must reevaluate their philosophies on formative data points, how they generate them, and how they apply them to their practice.

Both books focus on effectively using formative data in technology-driven, post–distance learning educational landscape with the ultimate goal of enhancing student learning and fostering equity. The companion book targets formative data on an organizational level with topics ranging from attendance to college preparedness, while this book discusses formative data in the classroom to inform instruction. They highlight connections to each other and emphasize strategies and best practices that apply to both, including opportunities to show how classroom formative data can inform organizational planning. Both books include:

- Implementation Tips on gathering formative data, differentiating support using technology, and collaboratively identifying and sharing best practices to maximize impact.
- Worksheets and tables to guide readers through the various steps of identifying and analyzing actionable formative data.
- Tech Tips to address logistical challenges and maximize instructional time.

- Formative Data for Social Justice features to ensure equity and access.
- Connections to organizational formative data companion book.

Part I: The Need to Reevaluate How We Use Data in the Classroom

Changing Instructional Data Considerations Due to . . . (Introduction)
- Advancements in Technology Changing Formative Data Use
- Loss of Consistent Summative Data From Previous Academic Years
- Concerns About Data Reliability Due to Increased Remote Assessment
- Concerns About "Learning Loss" During Distance Learning

NECESSITATE NEED TO REVISIT VISION

Your Classroom's Vision and Beliefs (Chapter 1)
- Assessing Your Classroom Vision
- Reflecting on Your Beliefs About Student Learning and Your Role
- Where Formative Data Fits In

WHICH GUIDE FORMATIVE DATA ROLE AND ITS IMPACT

The Impact of Formative Data on Student Success (Chapter 2)
- Formative Data Fosters Students' Growth Mindset
- Formative Data Informs Instruction
- Formative Data Facilitates Differentiation and Promotes Equity

FACILITATED BY

Part II: Effective Formative Data Use in the New Classroom

Maximizing the Effectiveness of Formative Data (Chapter 3)	Using Instructional Technology to Effectively Address Formative Data (Chapter 4)	Building Student Capacity Through Formative Data (Chapter 5)	Analyzing Formative Data Collaboratively to Identify and Celebrate Best Practices (Chapter 6)
◆ How *Actionable* Is the Data You Are Gathering? ◆ How *Timely* Is the Data You Are Gathering? ◆ How Much Data Do You Need?	◆ On-the-Fly Formative Data for Whole Class Instruction ◆ Formative Assessments for Differentiated Learning	◆ Digital Self-Assessment Rubrics ◆ Self-Selected Small Groups ◆ Self-Monitored Digital Success Trackers	◆ PLCs ◆ Peer Observations—In-Person and Virtual ◆ Teacher-Led Professional Development ◆ Success Celebration Events

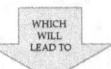
WHICH WILL LEAD TO

Innovative Learning in the New Classroom (Chapter 7)
- Re-envisioning Learning for All Students
- Reflecting on the Focus on Summative and Formative Assessments
- Preparing Students to Be Lifelong Independent Learners

Acknowledgments

I am eternally grateful to the people in my life who consistently supported and inspired me to give back to others. Writing this book would be impossible without the care and dedication of my parents, Vahe and Gretta, who instilled in me a love for learning from an early age. As immigrants fleeing a war-torn country, they emphasized that education in the United States would be the path to pursue my dreams, and I work every day to make that concept a reality for all students. I also want to thank my wife, Lara, whose steadfast encouragement and love helped me bring this book to life. I am also grateful to colleagues throughout my career in education who believed in me, challenged me to innovate and pursue opportunities to have a greater impact on student learning, and set an example for prioritizing students' success and well-being at all times. Their inspiration drives me to constantly push for new ways to advance student learning.

About the Author

Dr. Stepan Mekhitarian serves as the Director of Innovation, Instruction, Assessment, and Accountability for Glendale Unified School District, and he was one of the main leaders responsible for transitioning the large district to distance learning in response to the COVID-19 pandemic. Stepan previously served as the Coordinator of Data and Blended Learning in Los Angeles Unified School District. He has been passionate about instructional technology and data-driven decision making since his first year as a public school teacher. He has a wide breadth of experience in classroom and leadership positions and holds degrees from the University of California at Los Angeles, Harvard, and Loyola Marymount University (LMU). Stepan's doctoral research at LMU's Educational Leadership for Social Justice Program focused on the skills and training needed to effectively implement blended learning across schools and systems. He is a Google Certified Trainer, a Microsoft Innovative Educator, Blended Learning Universe Expert Advisor, and served as lecturer for the Instructional Technology for School Leaders course at LMU. In his spare time, he enjoys travel and spending time with his family and dog, Luna.

Part I
The Need to Reevaluate How We Use Data in the Classroom

Introduction
Changing Instructional Data Considerations

Part I: The Need to Reevaluate How We Use Data in the Classroom

Changing Instructional Data Considerations Due to ... *(Introduction)*
♦ Advancements in Technology Changing Formative Data Use
♦ Loss of Consistent Summative Data From Previous Academic Years
♦ Concerns About Data Reliability Due to Increased Remote Assessment
♦ Concerns About "Learning Loss" During Distance Learning

NECESSITATE NEED TO REVISIT VISION

Your Classroom's Vision and Beliefs *(Chapter 1)*
♦ Assessing Your Classroom Vision
♦ Reflecting on Your Beliefs About Student Learning and Your Role
♦ Where Formative Data Fits In

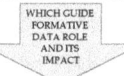
WHICH GUIDE FORMATIVE DATA ROLE AND ITS IMPACT

The Impact of Formative Data on Student Success *(Chapter 2)*
♦ Formative Data Fosters Students' Growth Mindset
♦ Formative Data Informs Instruction
♦ Formative Data Facilitates Differentiation and Promotes Equity

FACILITATED BY

Part II: Effective Formative Data Use in the New Classroom

Maximizing the Effectiveness of Formative Data *(Chapter 3)*	Using Instructional Technology to Effectively Address Formative Data *(Chapter 4)*	Building Student Capacity Through Formative Data *(Chapter 5)*	Analyzing Formative Data Collaboratively to Identify and Celebrate Best Practices *(Chapter 6)*
♦ How *Actionable* Is the Data You Are Gathering? ♦ How *Timely* Is the Data You Are Gathering? ♦ How Much Data Do You Need?	♦ On-the-Fly Formative Data for Whole Class Instruction ♦ Formative Assessments for Differentiated Learning	♦ Digital Self-Assessment Rubrics ♦ Self-Selected Small Groups ♦ Self-Monitored Digital Success Trackers	♦ PLCs ♦ Peer Observations—In-Person and Virtual ♦ Teacher-Led Professional Development ♦ Success Celebration Events

DOI: 10.4324/9781003246213-2

Innovative Learning in the New Classroom *(Chapter 7)*
♦ Re-envisioning Learning for All Students
♦ Reflecting on the Focus on Summative and Formative Assessments
♦ Preparing Students to Be Lifelong Independent Learners

In recent years, the collection, analysis, and application of formative data has shifted due to advancements in technology, availability of data, and understanding of the impact of formative data on student achievement. Increased access to data has been a double-edged sword, offering more data points than ever to analyze but also making it more challenging to navigate the sea of data to target the topics that are most critical and actionable. This trend was suddenly upended by the unexpected transition to distance learning because of the COVID-19 pandemic. The consistent flow of data points was disrupted and academic performance, attendance, discipline, and other measures were all impacted by the shift. For many districts, schools reopening signals a return to traditional data analysis plans and a "picking up where we left off" approach to data points going back to 2019. This move, however, is a tremendous missed opportunity for two reasons:

1. It is not every day that we have a chance to reset and rethink our entire philosophy around data analysis and action. The distance learning experience offers a once-in-a-lifetime chance to reflect upon and reevaluate how we do things, and we must take advantage of this opportunity.
2. The distance learning experience served as a "technology boot camp" for educators, dramatically increasing their technical expertise in a short amount of time; we can capitalize on this newfound skillset to change the way we access and use formative data.

By taking advantage of this opportunity to reflect and reset using our expanded experience with technology, we can forever alter how we gather and use actionable data points to impact student achievement. All we need is a desire to innovate and build on our experience. Change is never easy, especially when it impacts how things have been done for a long time and requires buy-in from multiple stakeholder groups in order to be meaningful. Later in this book, we will explore how to solicit engagement from school administrators, while the companion book—*Harnessing Formative Data for K-12 Leaders*—discusses buy-in at the organizational level.

••

The distance learning experience offers a once-in-a-lifetime chance to reflect upon and reevaluate how we do things, and we must take advantage of this opportunity.

••

The changes to how we view data are driven in many ways by the dramatic impact distance learning had on the educational landscape. The unexpected transition to distance learning pushed educators to reflect on how they typically use data and consider alternative approaches. These updates are driven by:

♦ Advancements in technology.
♦ The loss of consistent summative data from previous academic years.
♦ Concerns about data reliability due to increased remote assessment.
♦ Concerns about "learning loss" during distance learning.

As each played a role in guiding our thinking about data in the classroom, it is important to understand the impact of each before we explore the possibilities of a new approach.

Advancements in Technology Changing Formative Data Use

Consider how instructional technology has advanced over the past decade and how much technical expertise educators have gathered over the past few years; the educational landscape is ready for a giant leap forward in data analysis and action. Said et al. (2019) states, "Growing technological advancement has prompted a paradigm shift from traditional forms like paper tests to technology-enhanced assessments for the digital natives in our 21st Century classrooms" (p. 26). These advancements in technology offer two main benefits for enhanced data analysis in the classroom: ease of access to actionable data, and real-time access to formative data. Ease of access ensures more frequent use of data points as they become more convenient to access and apply, while real-time access increases the likelihood that the data points will more directly impact students' needs at that moment to continue their progress toward mastery. This level of access, however, will require training and practice to master. When should teachers access this formative data? How often should data be gathered and accessed? What should be done with the data? Luckin et al. (2017) explain,

> [Learning analytics] offers a strong example of how technology offers unique opportunities for assessment. However, the potential of these opportunities to be met will depend greatly on teachers' ability to structure effective inquiry activities to probe the rich data sets that technology can afford.
>
> Technology can support assessment for learning by providing tools to traffic in assessment interactions: potentially making them more prompt, representationally rich, and interactive, but only if teachers become fluent in using the available technological tools to inquire about their students' learning. (p. 92)

As we dig deeper into implementing real-time formative data use using technology, we will discuss how to redesign your classroom vision to incorporate data analysis efficiently to see significant gains in student achievement. This vision will need to be closely tied to equity and access concepts that are at the core of any social justice–focused classroom and the drivers for differentiated instruction and supports. They will be critical themes throughout this book and will be the focus of the culminating re-envisioned classroom described in the last chapter.

Before we go much further, let us come to a common understanding about formative data and formative assessments. Formative data points are gathered by the teacher and inform planning and next steps. These data points can come from a wide variety of questions, surveys, assessments, mini-projects, and other sources. Regardless of their format, formative data points must lead to adjustments to the lesson; otherwise, they are simply checks without action. Also, note that informing next steps is the purpose of the data points; they should not be used for grades or as any other type of formal assessment. Finally, as we will explore later in this book, formative data points will ideally inform both the teacher *and* the students about areas of strength and focus to promote independent learning. Note that formative assessments differ from summative assessments; formative assessments are assessments *for* learning, while summative assessments are assessments *of* learning. Summative assessments give students an opportunity to demonstrate what they have learned, but not before you have had opportunities to provide differentiated supports using formative assessments. Ideally, summative assessments are given when the formative assessments suggest that students are ready, transforming summative assessments from a dreaded event to an opportunity to demonstrate success and celebrate the results. They do not need to be given on set dates established at the start of the school year.

Regardless of their format, formative data points must lead to adjustments to the lesson; otherwise, they are simply checks without action.

 CONNECTION TO COMPANION BOOK

Technology has changed the way we gather and analyze actionable formative data, both in the classroom and at the organizational level. Though the timeline and application of formative data look a little different at the two levels, they both serve to inform planning, initiatives, and supports. The companion book explores the impact of technology on data analysis at the organizational level in more detail.

Instructional Technology Creates New Opportunities to Gather and Use Data

Imagine being able to know exactly what your students understand and what questions they still have. How would that impact your instruction? Would you continue teaching the lesson as you had initially planned, or would you make continuous adjustments based on this information? What impact would this information have on student success? While this type of detailed insight may sound like fantasy, we can get closer to that vision of the classroom now more than ever due to advances in classroom technology. Consider how technology can help access actionable data, both in terms of effort and timeliness. A classroom with easy-to-access and near-instant formative data is possible, though both training and thoughtful planning are necessary to make it a reality. Chanpet et al. (2018) explain, "No assessment technology is in itself formative, but almost any assessment technology can be used in a formative way" (p. 702). This insistence on consistently looking for formative data to inform instruction and planning nudges us closer than ever to that ideal classroom environment we imagined.

Some instructional technology tools you can use to quickly and timely access formative data include ungraded assessments and surveys on computers or phones, online platforms that include formative assessment apps such as Kahoot and Nearpod, and open-ended formative data through sites like Google Jamboard and AnswerGarden. Kahoot and Nearpod allow students to answer questions in real-time to give you information about progress; Kahoot is typically set up in a gamified format where time to response plays a role in points, while Nearpod can seamlessly incorporate questions into a slidedeck to allow you to stop and check for understanding during direct instruction. Google Jamboard and AnswerGarden, on the other hand, both offer variations on an open-ended response board that allows users to type a response to a prompt and allow you to see all the responses at once. In Google Jamboard, students type their responses on virtual "sticky notes" and post them to the page, which can facilitate extended thinking as they can post their notes in different places based on your prompts. AnswerGarden is unique in that it magnifies the size of responses that are repeated, offering a terrific visual representation of the frequency of each response. The more popular a response, the larger the font for that response becomes. Another option is the slidedeck approach in which you create a collaborative slidedeck using a program like Google Slides and have each student or group respond to the same prompt on a separate slide; you can then review multiple responses quickly, identify patterns in the responses, and give students opportunities to easily review other groups' responses and provide feedback (we'll review the process for implementing this strategy in more detail in Chapter 5).

Each of these programs offers formative data you can use to gather insight on student mastery and adjust your instruction accordingly. As always, choosing the best option comes down to how you intend to use the data. For example, quick checks for understanding during direct instruction to inform small group review may work best with Nearpod. On the other hand,

Jamboard may be the ideal tool to use when you want to see student responses on one sheet and then make connections between them to advance learning. You can move responses around the page, add lines to connect them, and ask students to circle the notes they have questions about; the possibilities are endless.

While each option shares the common benefit of offering quick and timely feedback, it requires thoughtful planning in terms of building the assessments and determining what will be done with the data once it is collected. These planning elements are critical for getting ever closer to that visionary classroom in which we know how to provide personalized support and learning for each student. As we dive deeper into planning how to use the formative data gathered, keep in mind that different formative assessments will offer different levels of action. Some formative assessments will give you information on each student's performance to help you individually differentiate supports, while others will offer insights on how to adjust instructions for small groups or the entire class. A variety of formative assessment formats ensures that you have access to insights to realistically inform your planning. Use Figure I.1 to reflect on the instructional technology resources you currently use and what type of formative data they provide.

If you listed a variety of resources that offer differing levels of action and consistently offer easy-to-access data, you are well on your way to making that visionary classroom a reality. Remember that differentiation is key for equitable access to supports; equity differs from equality in that equity provides students with whatever they need to succeed, even if those supports differ from the ones provided to other students. Therefore, conversations about differentiation and equity go hand in hand, regardless of the classroom setting or subject. Our efforts to differentiate using formative data points to meet students' needs ultimately serve to further equity in the classroom. In this book, we will examine how to incorporate these programs into a comprehensive instructional plan that builds on student mastery and provides targeted support based on data.

FIGURE I.1 Reflection on Current Formative Data Collection Using Technology

Technology-based program/site you use for formative data	Level of action it offers (individual, small group, etc.)	Describe its ease of access and timeliness

TECH TIP

In Chapter 4, we will explore the importance of creating a formative data platform that efficiently collects and houses data points to minimize logistical challenges in order to maximize time for analysis and next steps. Consider what platform you will use to simplify access to data and best practices, including whether your student information system has the capability for this project.

Identifying *Actionable* Data From a Sea of Data Points

One of the challenges we experience as educators in the 21st century is navigating through an overabundance of technology. It is a time of tremendous innovation with new resources regularly being offered and constant updates to existing technology. You probably receive multiple emails each day introducing new instructional technology for your classroom. For most educators, the classroom they teach in looks nothing like the classroom they learned in as students, and very few of the resources they used as students persist in their same form today. With so many advancements in technology, the amount of data we have access to has increased exponentially as well. How can we possibly be expected to keep up with all the data points we have access to? In many ways, this is a good problem to have; an abundance of data points gives us the option to choose which ones we focus on as long as we can navigate the sea of data points.

I faced this challenge not only as a classroom teacher but also as the Director of Innovation, Instruction, Assessment & Accountability at Glendale Unified School District. As the data lead for the district, my responsibilities included providing school sites with data points to show their progress on a variety of metrics. It was an interesting position to be in, especially since I had access to virtually any data point available to the district. Although I could provide large reports to schools with comprehensive data points, I chose instead to prioritize sharing data points that were *actionable*. The "why" behind every data point drove the conversations to ensure data analysis efforts consistently enhanced student progress. Informative data points were shared to show overall progress and provide insights on successes and areas of growth, but the majority of our discussions focused on actionable data points and potential next steps to address them. As educators, there must be a sense of urgency around our work as our time with each student is limited; we must focus on information that can help us improve students' learning. If unsure about which data points to prioritize, pick the ones that will most directly inform your next steps.

••
Conversations about differentiation and equity go hand in hand, regardless of the classroom setting or subject.
••

> **FORMATIVE DATA FOR SOCIAL JUSTICE**
>
> To close the achievement gap, students who are behind grade level need to maximize instructional time. Assessments can impact instructional time, so any time devoted to them must serve to inform and improve instruction. Formative assessments that include prompts that do not inform next steps can negatively impact achievement because they take time away from learning without contributing insights to learning. Ensure all prompts result in actionable data points so all students get the support needed to succeed. We will explore this concept further in Chapter 3.

Loss of Consistent Summative Data From Previous Academic Years

Before the COVID-19 pandemic, our district's schools used to plan for the upcoming school year by using the summative data from the previous year to identify areas of focus. The strategy offered an effective approach to basing focus areas on evidence with the understanding that formative data would be gathered throughout the year to gauge progress toward those focus areas. The pandemic effectively paused traditional summative assessments and accountability measures, creating a void where schools expected to see prior year data. In the absence of prior year summative data points, schools were forced to base their instructional plans on current year formative data, pushing them to place a heavier emphasis on real-time data from formative assessments. Though this change in approach was driven by unexpectedly unavailable information, it was a reminder that circumstances can change at any time, so being well-versed on gathering and utilizing real-time data is critical and hard to beat for consistency and applicability.

CONNECTION TO COMPANION BOOK

Data points from the prior year may not always be readily available or reliable, as was the case during the pandemic. In the absence of prior year data points, there is a heightened focus on formative data from the current year, both in the classroom and at the organizational level. The companion book focuses on using formative data during regular intervals to inform the work of leadership teams, while this book stresses the importance of using current year formative data daily to inform instruction and planning.

Continuity of Data Points Disrupted by Changing Events

The lack of prior year summative data also created a break in continuity for a variety of data reports we are used to reviewing. Summative data points on academic performance, attendance, and other metrics were all disrupted as a result of the transition to distance learning stemming from the pandemic. This change was sudden and interrupted the traditional data review discussions we are used to, but we can view this disruption as a unique opportunity to rethink how we look at data points and how we think about actionable data over multiple years. Many schools shifted their focus to current year formative data points instead of prior year summative data points, heightening the timeliness and actionability of data-driven instructional planning. It may be frustrating to not have access to the data points we are used to reviewing, but the chance to reflect and rethink on how we use data is a great blessing in disguise. It can validate elements of previous practices while pushing us to find alternatives and potential improvements.

Continuity of Data Points Disrupted by Changing Standards

Even without changes stemming from the transition to distance learning, multi-year data analysis has always been at the mercy of changing standards, metrics, dashboards, and other factors that impact how we look at data. Looking at these metrics with a critical lens is essential for assessing progress, but their inconsistency over the years is a powerful reminder that few are as effective as real-time formative data points, which are never outdated and arguably have the greatest likelihood of leading to actionable next steps to improve student learning. Prioritizing them over summative assessments takes some getting used to, but the potential benefits are vast and worth starting conversations around. Regardless of changes that come, formative data points always remain relevant.

Concerns About Data Reliability Due to Increased Remote Assessment

A recurring concern that frequently appeared in discussions about best practices during distance learning was the validity of data from assessments. Teachers expressed skepticism about the validity of assessment data as students had access to unauthorized supports at home. There are two ways we recommended addressing this concern, both of which expanded the impact of formative assessments. First, we advocated for increased formative assessment use over summative assessment in the distance learning space, reducing the number of "high-stakes" assessments and instead shifting the focus to learning instead of grades. Second, we encouraged utilizing higher-order questions on formative assessments, which require analysis and cannot be simply found online. This combination of rigorous questioning with a focus on learning and growth is a powerful way to shift how we traditionally view assessments.

••

The term "learning loss" was coined in anticipation of reduced learning opportunities that would stem from distance learning, but maximizing learning through formative data to inform instruction and planning keeps the focus on actionable next steps.

••

Concerns About "Learning Loss" During Distance Learning

Very early on into the distance learning experience, the phrase "learning loss" became popularized to describe the presumed limited learning that was taking place. Deep concern by students, teachers, and parents/guardians dominated conversations about what students were learning during distance learning, what they were missing out on, and how we would help them "catch up" and avoid the dreaded "learning loss." In our district, however, we refrained from adopting this term and instead viewed this experience as a "maximizing learning opportunity." Understanding that instructional time was more precious than ever with limited synchronous learning each day during distance learning, we focused on maximizing learning by focusing on student needs, which were driven by formative data. The term "learning loss" was coined in anticipation of reduced learning opportunities that would stem from distance learning, but maximizing learning through formative data to inform instruction and planning keeps the focus on actionable next steps. The learning format, whether distance or in-person, does not determine learning gain or loss alone. Once again, heavy emphasis falls on the importance of personalizing learning using data-informed decision-making.

IMPLEMENTATION TIP

Consider the connotations of the term "learning loss," which was popularized during the transition to distance learning. It can be interpreted to suggest that teaching simply wasn't as effective across the board during distance learning, which may not be accurate. In fact, some students thrived in the distance learning setting. Use a positive term instead of one based on loss, such as "maximizing learning." This will reinforce the notion that we are constantly looking for ways to enhance learning regardless of the learning environment or platform, an important distinction to further our commitment to growth mindset.

Key Takeaways

In this chapter, we explored the changing instructional data landscape due to technology expansion, the COVID-19 pandemic, and other factors in order to better understand the environment in which we will be utilizing data to drive instruction. Regardless of the factor considered, one truth remained constant: there is no substitute for the powerful impact of formative data points gathered and used regularly. Advancements in technology enhance the ease of access and timeliness of the data, which require training to maximize. The loss of consistent summative data from previous academic years, concerns about data reliability due to increased remote assessment, and concerns about "learning loss" during distance learning can all be countered with heightened and carefully designed formative assessments. As we dive into innovative ways to rethink real-time formative data, keep that dream classroom in mind, a classroom in which students all receive the support and instruction they need based on progress toward mastery. Your classroom vision, which we will develop in the next chapter, will be key in bringing that classroom to life.

Your Classroom's Vision and Beliefs

Part I: The Need to Reevaluate How We Use Data in the Classroom

Changing Instructional Data Considerations Due to . . . *(Introduction)*
♦ Advancements in Technology Changing Formative Data Use
♦ Loss of Consistent Summative Data From Previous Academic Years
♦ Concerns About Data Reliability Due to Increased Remote Assessment
♦ Concerns About "Learning Loss" During Distance Learning

NECESSITATE NEED TO REVISIT VISION

Your Classroom's Vision and Beliefs *(Chapter 1)*
♦ Assessing Your Classroom Vision
♦ Reflecting on Your Beliefs About Student Learning and Your Role
♦ Where Formative Data Fits In

WHICH GUIDE FORMATIVE DATA ROLE AND ITS IMPACT

The Impact of Formative Data on Student Success *(Chapter 2)*
♦ Formative Data Fosters Students' Growth Mindset
♦ Formative Data Informs Instruction
♦ Formative Data Facilitates Differentiation and Promotes Equity

DOI: 10.4324/9781003246213-3

Part II: Effective Formative Data Use in the New Classroom

Maximizing the Effectiveness of Formative Data (Chapter 3)	Using Instructional Technology to Effectively Address Formative Data (Chapter 4)	Building Student Capacity Through Formative Data (Chapter 5)	Analyzing Formative Data Collaboratively to Identify and Celebrate Best Practices (Chapter 6)
♦ How *Actionable* Is the Data You Are Gathering? ♦ How *Timely* Is the Data You Are Gathering? ♦ How Much Data Do You Need?	♦ On-the-Fly Formative Data for Whole Class Instruction ♦ Formative Assessments for Differentiated Learning	♦ Digital Self-Assessment Rubrics ♦ Self-Selected Small Groups ♦ Self-Monitored Digital Success Trackers	♦ PLCs ♦ Peer Observations—In-Person and Virtual ♦ Teacher-Led Professional Development ♦ Success Celebration Events

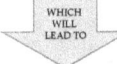

Innovative Learning in the New Classroom (Chapter 7)
♦ Re-envisioning Learning for All Students ♦ Reflecting on the Focus on Summative and Formative Assessments ♦ Preparing Students to Be Lifelong Independent Learners

Assessing Your Classroom Vision

Think of classrooms you entered as a student years ago—did you feel the same as you entered each room? What are some characteristics of classes you have fond memories of long after you have graduated? What did the teacher say or do to make you remember the course so well after many years? Each teacher has the power to set the tone for the classroom that will ultimately shape how students feel in their ability to be engaged, inquisitive, and successful. That classroom culture comes from the vision you establish and the educational philosophy you adopt.

Take a moment to reflect on your current classroom vision. How would students describe your classroom? What would they say is your goal as a teacher? Would all students in the classroom share a similar response? What factors could result in varying responses? There is no perfect classroom vision and that is ok; as educators, we just need to continue to grow, reflect, revise, and adapt to continuously make our classroom a center that is student-centered, inclusive, and focused on equitable access to learning. Consider what is important to you and why you decided to become a teacher in the first place to drive your thinking.

A vision that prioritizes students' growth mindset is essential for building their capacity as lifelong learners and requires a clear plan for gathering and utilizing formative data. This vision encourages students to push themselves to learn, to develop an understanding of what they have mastered and what they are still working on, and how to seek support to make progress toward mastery. We will explore how formative data can help foster students' growth mindset in the next chapter.

In addition to the focus on growth mindset, your classroom culture should employ constructivist elements to engage students and facilitate meaning making and discovery through conversations and collaborations that encourage students to share their perspectives and backgrounds. This approach, which helps students "make meaning" through a discovery process, helps students internalize their learning and make connections that ultimately support understanding. Not only does this help connect students to the content and to each other, it reinforces the notion of equity in the classroom as students' backgrounds are shared and celebrated. Constructivism in your instructional plan dramatically creates access by eliminating systemic barriers to learning that are often built into our education system. For example, instead of reading about a problem on horseback riding, which only some students may be familiar with, you can ask students to describe the first time they saw someone on a horse, whether it was on a ranch or in a movie. They can share from their experience at that moment with others and apply their unique perspectives to a problem about horseback riding. Collaboratively tackling the problem can enhance rigor by creating opportunities for students to address the problem together through different lenses. The end result will be a more robust solution, and the process better prepares them for problem-solving as adults.

I discuss the importance of incorporating constructivism into classroom practices in my book on post-pandemic instructional technology use: *The Essential Blended Learning PD Planner: Where Classroom Practice Meets Distance Learning* (2021). A constructivist learning approach can create additional opportunities for formative assessment in various formats. When designing their research study on the impact of formative assessment using technology, Cusi et al. (2017) explain that

> The perspective adopted on teaching—learning processes influences the ways in which [formative assessment] may be activated with the support of technology. Our study is based on a Vygotskyan perspective (Vygotsky, 1978), in which interaction with peers and experts plays a crucial role in students' learning. (p. 756)

A classroom vision that fosters students' growth mindset through formative data generated by constructivist learning opportunities and effective instructional technology use has the power to transform students' lives long after they have left your classroom.

CONNECTION TO COMPANION BOOK

The companion book explores the development of an organizational vision that promotes growth mindset, equity, and a desire to become lifelong learners through the use of formative data. These should be connected to the vision in each classroom that promotes the same goals. If classrooms and boardrooms are sharing the same message about the vision for student learning, one will enhance the other and lead to greater success. Coherence across the organization builds on strengths and accelerates progress toward mastery, so work on developing buy-in instead of choosing to work in isolation in your classroom.

Your vision can also lead to a visualization of what your classroom will look like for students. Imagine what a truly incredible learning experience looks like and then what type of vision would need to be in place in that classroom. During professional development, I often ask teachers and school leaders to have a conversation and jot down on Google Jamboard what the "perfect" classroom would look like if resources were not a factor. I do not define "perfect" and ask them to be as ambitious as they can with an unlimited budget. However, I ask them to be very detailed in their responses, specifically:

- What a teacher is doing and saying in a "perfect" classroom.
- What students are saying and doing in a "perfect" classroom.
- What a visitor might see as soon as they open the door to a "perfect" classroom.

Without exception, I get some variation of the same responses: students are collaborating and highly engaged, there is differentiated small group instruction, technology is being used, formative data is visualized on the walls, the teacher is largely playing the role of a facilitator, and students are not all doing the same thing. Consistently, their vision of the ideal learning environment is one facilitated by a blended learning approach. With the rapid expansion of technical expertise for teachers and students, this may be the right time to adopt an instructional technology-led approach to facilitate learning. Schmitz (2019) explains,

> A challenge for students in a flipped environment is their low level of self-regulation (Iwamoto et al., 2017). Self-directed learning is essential for students in a flipped classroom. While this may seem a high-risk proposition, today's students are surprisingly well equipped. (p. 2)

Our students are more ready than ever for a new learning environment that maximizes the benefits of instructional technology, especially after their distance learning experience.

•••

Technology is not a silver bullet that will immediately advance learning upon implementation; it is a resource not unlike textbooks and manipulatives that educators can utilize in a well-designed lesson.

•••

Consider a blended learning model that uses instructional technology to personalize learning and facilitate students' growth mindset. The flipped classroom model in which new content is introduced at home through readings and teacher-recorded videos and class time is used for collaboration, discussion, and application is a particularly strong model to facilitate formative data use. Regardless of which model you adopt, build your classroom around a philosophy that puts students first by building their capacity and honoring their unique perspectives and backgrounds. This means students' growth mindset uses formative data to provide feedback and customized supports to students, consistently moving them toward mastery. Note that technology is not a silver bullet that will immediately advance learning upon implementation; it is a resource not unlike textbooks and manipulatives that educators can utilize in a well-designed lesson. Ultimately, the teacher—not technology—determines the effectiveness of learning opportunities. Applying technology thoughtfully can enhance your efforts by facilitating greater collaboration, differentiation, and inquiry. Consider how you will establish this type of vision using Figure 1.1.

Keep in mind that an effective vision will focus on the student experience and will be framed from the perspective of student success, not teacher action. Describe how *students* will feel in your class and what they will do. Reflect on specific students you taught and how the differentiated supports you provided ultimately resulted in their success. That specific targeting of their needs may have made the difference between success and failure. Think about students who have reached out to you

FIGURE 1.1 Developing Your Classroom Vision

	How will your classroom vision do each of the following?
Foster students' growth mindset	
Promote constructivist thinking	
Incorporate technology to enhance learning	

to thank you for your efforts after graduation. Recall students who could have benefited from differentiated supports, possibly students during your initial years as a teacher while you were developing your craft. These experiences can help you internalize the challenges students face as leaders and how a focused effort on meeting the needs of *all* students through differentiation can have a lasting impact on their educational journey.

Be sure to place heavy emphasis on ensuring all students in class receive equitable support and importance. Consider the needs of different student groups. A vision must apply to *all* students in the classroom, and all students will not benefit from its promise if equity is not front and center. A classroom vision that prioritizes equity and promotes *all* students' success is one that should be celebrated, studied, and replicated. Review the approaches you developed in Figure 1.1 to describe a classroom vision that puts the student experience first and fosters equity, and summarize them in Figure 1.2.

FORMATIVE DATA FOR SOCIAL JUSTICE

Equity and access for all students, regardless of the demographic composition of your classroom, must be a critical element of your classroom vision. Students have varying learning modalities and backgrounds, and your vision must include language that commits to serving all students.

FIGURE 1.2 Your Equitable Classroom Vision

> Summarize your vision statement that prioritizes equity in the space below. Be sure to incorporate how the vision:
> - Fosters students' growth mindset
> - Promotes constructivist thinking
> - Incorporates technology to enhance learning

Use this vision to inform your thinking as you continue to explore your role in the classroom and formative data. Consider how, if at all, the distance learning experience impacted your classroom vision and your role in the classroom. The distance learning experience gave teachers an unprecedented view into students' lives at home and pushed teachers to explore new teaching methodologies and utilize new resources—will these impact your new classroom vision?

....

An effective vision will focus on the student experience and will be framed from the perspective of student success, not teacher action. Describe how *students* will feel in your class and what they will do.

....

Reflecting on Your Beliefs About Student Learning and Your Role

An equity-based vision that fosters students' growth mindset and promotes constructivist thinking is one that builds students' capacity as independent learners; students can make meaning by bringing in their own experiences and learn to develop the belief that they can continuously learn and grow. As students become independent learners, what does the teacher role look like? In order for students to grow as independent learners, they must take ownership of their learning, and that can only happen if the teacher creates opportunities for them to do this. This approach entails creating learning opportunities that encourage exploration, analysis, collaboration, and consistent, constructive feedback to move students toward mastery and to provide individualized differentiation. A great approach for including these learning opportunities is to utilize project-based learning, or PBL. Project-based learning allows students to understand and apply a wide variety of skills and concepts in the context of an explorative project. To ensure steady progress toward learning and mastery, the teacher's role is to provide scaffolded, personalized support and guidance to allow students to develop their independence as learners. Chanpet et al. (2018) explain:

> Instead of teaching, instructing or transmitting knowledge, the instructor scaffolds the complex activity and interactions that occur in PBL [project-based learning]. Scaffolding means offering support "for tasks or concepts that the "student is initially unable to grasp on his/her own . . ." (van Rooij, 2009). Scaffolding is an approach to formative assessment. Formative assessment is an integral part of [problem-based learning or PBL] (Gulbahar & Tinmaz, 2006) and means that assessment occurs during and following PBL (Solomon, 2003) or, as Gikandi et al. (2011) recommended, embedded "within the learning process" (p. 2348). In forms of PBL that follow specific steps or phases, scaffolding, formative assessment and feedback given to teams and individual learners can help them to move progressively through each step towards the final goal of the project and co-construction of the associated artifacts. (p. 686)

The teacher needs a steady stream of information about student understanding, inquiries, and concerns to provide this support. This is precisely where our expanded instructional technology expertise can fit in, offering resources to gather real-time, actionable data to inform support. These data points are particularly helpful in identifying misconceptions through the introduction of distractors. Sahin (2019) explains, "the instructors can provide information about the item difficulty and item discrimination, or information about distractors. And also, the systems can provide feedback to learners about individual shortcomings" (p. 694). Technology itself does not provide actionable data; it merely facilitates the efficient and timely collection of it. Troy and Bulgakov-Cooke (2013) explain:

> The remarkable potential for using new technologies, such as SMART Boards and related instructional software, should be developed by instructional leaders and embraced by teachers. However, no tool in and of itself will embody the fundamental value and practice of formative assessment. It is up to teachers and students to act intentionally as proponents of learning, regardless of which technologies may or may not be available at a given time. Formative assessment is as old as the art of teaching and does not depend on new devices; it should be understood on its own terms before specific tools are relied on to enact it. (p. 26)

With thoughtful, equitable opportunities that facilitate independent learning, the teacher can incorporate data-driven scaffolding and supports using technology to ensure all students succeed. This is the type of classroom that should result from your vision. It cannot come to fruition, however, without consistent access to actionable formative data.

••

In order for students to grow as independent learners, they must take ownership of their learning, and that can only happen if the teacher creates opportunities for them to do this.

••

> **IMPLEMENTATION TIP**
>
> Many students will not understand the purpose of formative assessments and how you intend to use them when they join your classroom. Be transparent with them and explain how formative assessments will inform your planning. Share with them that you intend to develop their self-monitoring skills using formative assessments so they become independent learners. Remind them that building this skill will prepare them for a bright future, and even though they will become independent learners, they will have your support and guidance along the way.

Where Formative Data Fits In

With your vision for equity guiding your instructional approach, determine how formative data will fit into your plan. Formative data points will provide the insights needed to identify student needs, provide differentiated supports, and inform planning. They permeate virtually all facets of classroom planning and practice and must be an integral part of any successful pedagogical approach. Cusi et al. (2017) explain,

> There are five key strategies for [formative assessment] practices in school settings, according to Wiliam and Thompson (2007): (a) clarifying and sharing learning intentions and criteria for success; (b) engineering effective classroom discussions and other learning tasks that elicit evidence of student understanding; (c) providing feedback that moves learners forward; (d) activating students as instructional resources for one another; (e) activating students as the owners of their own learning. The teacher, student's peers and the student him- or herself are the agents that activate these [formative assessment] strategies. (p. 176)

A vision focused on equitable learning for all and delivered through formative data use can be transformative. Imagine being a student in a classroom with a strong focus on formative assessment through these five strategies:

- You know what you're learning, why you are learning it, and how you will prove you learned it.
- You know you'll have several opportunities to explore the topic with your classmates and develop a deeper understanding.
- You know you will receive constructive feedback to help you build on your understanding.
- You know that you will be able to give and receive support from others.
- You know that you will continue to develop as an independent learner and better understand your strengths and areas of focus.

A student in this setting feels encouraged and successful—even when they have not yet achieved mastery—because they know the focus is on learning, and they have multiple opportunities to demonstrate mastery. However, Vasquez et al. (2017) explain,

> Despite the benefits of formative assessment, its use in the classroom is far from widespread (Shute & Kim, 2014). This is partly due to the fact that formative assessment requires teachers to obtain and analyze information on student learning from several sources and in a short space of time. (p. 1143)

With effective technology use, however, these supports can be delivered more frequently, and formative data use can become more commonplace. Increased use of technology can also increase the accuracy of data points needed to make informed instructional decisions. Shirley and Irving (2014) explain, "In the absence of accurate data, teachers may use less reliable data to infer what students do and do not understand" (p. 62), while Onodipe and Ayadi (2020) emphasize the benefits of using technology in the classroom to inform planning, stating,

> Smartphones can be used in the classroom for formative assessment. Quizzes conducted in class during the learning process are useful to the professor because they provide a chance to determine what students understand and where there is confusion. Armed with this information, the professor can modify teaching activities to improve student learning. (p. 5)

TECH TIP

Consider traditional formative assessments and whether technology can enhance them. Prompts that students respond to on personal whiteboards can be replaced with keyword sites like AnswerGarden, but does this transition enhance the learning experience? If the transition to a technology-based approach improves efficiency or provides more robust data, then it may be worth the leap. Otherwise, keeping traditional formative assessment approaches may be the better step forward.

Bringing these ideas together shows us the potential impact a carefully crafted vision can have on student achievement. It can be challenging to set a vision that takes them all into consideration, but the benefits of the process are well worth it. In the next chapter, we will examine some of the impacts more closely, but for now, let's bring together these ideas as one visualization in Figure 1.3.

FIGURE 1.3 Bring Together the Elements Needed for Your Classroom Vision

An equity-driven classroom vision

⬇ THAT

• Fosters students' growth mindset. • Promotes constructivist thinking.

⬇ NECESSITATES

A reevaluation of the teacher's role in the classroom as a facilitator who • Builds students' capacity as independent learners. • Adjusts instruction and supports using formative data.

⬇ USING

Technology to accelerate and enhance both steps.

Revisit your established vision in Figure 1.2 and reflect on any updates that may be necessary to capture all of these critical elements. In the subsequent chapters, referencing your vision will be essential to creating a plan that centers on formative data.

FORMATIVE DATA FOR SOCIAL JUSTICE

Reevaluating your role in the classroom around a growth mindset and independent learner vision is one of the biggest steps you can take to furthering social justice in your classroom. Students who have traditionally not been given an opportunity to take ownership of their learning may be surprised by this change at first, but their growth as learners will be swift with your support. Update your role in your classroom, and you may change their success trajectory for the rest of their lives.

Key Takeaways

In this chapter, we examined how your classroom vision informs your approach to equity, instruction, and planning and what role formative data points play in bringing your vision to life. In the next chapter, we will look more closely into how formative data points foster students' growth mindset, inform instruction, and facilitate differentiation. With that understanding, we will be ready to jump into effective formative data practices you will be able to implement using instructional technology.

2

The Impact of Formative Data on Student Success

Part I: The Need to Reevaluate How We Use Data in the Classroom

Changing Instructional Data Considerations Due to . . . *(Introduction)*
♦ Advancements in Technology Changing Formative Data Use
♦ Loss of Consistent Summative Data From Previous Academic Years
♦ Concerns About Data Reliability Due to Increased Remote Assessment
♦ Concerns About "Learning Loss" During Distance Learning

Your Classroom's Vision and Beliefs *(Chapter 1)*
♦ Assessing Your Classroom Vision
♦ Reflecting on Your Beliefs About Student Learning and Your Role
♦ Where Formative Data Fits In

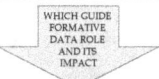

The Impact of Formative Data on Student Success *(Chapter 2)*
♦ Formative Data Fosters Students' Growth Mindset
♦ Formative Data Informs Instruction
♦ Formative Data Facilitates Differentiation and Promotes Equity

DOI: 10.4324/9781003246213-4

Part II: Effective Formative Data Use in the New Classroom

Maximizing the Effectiveness of Formative Data (*Chapter 3*)	Using Instructional Technology to Effectively Address Formative Data (*Chapter 4*)	Building Student Capacity Through Formative Data (*Chapter 5*)	Analyzing Formative Data Collaboratively to Identify and Celebrate Best Practices (*Chapter 6*)
♦ How *Actionable* Is the Data You Are Gathering? ♦ How *Timely* Is the Data You Are Gathering? ♦ How Much Data Do You Need?	♦ On-the-Fly Formative Data for Whole Class Instruction ♦ Formative Assessments for Differentiated Learning	♦ Digital Self-Assessment Rubrics ♦ Self-Selected Small Groups ♦ Self-Monitored Digital Success Trackers	♦ PLCs ♦ Peer Observations—In-Person and Virtual ♦ Teacher-Led Professional Development ♦ Success Celebration Events

Innovative Learning in the New Classroom (*Chapter 7*)
♦ Re-envisioning Learning for All Students ♦ Reflecting on the Focus on Summative and Formative Assessments ♦ Preparing Students to Be Lifelong Independent Learners

Formative Data Fosters Students' Growth Mindset

In the previous chapter, we briefly touched on how formative data points and the supports and interventions that result from them can build students' growth mindset, which is critical for development as lifelong learners. I learned the importance of developing students' growth mindset early in my career as a high school math teacher from an experience with a student named "John." John had a well-documented learning disability and made it a point during the first week of school to let me know that he would fail my class because he "had never been good at math." I told him his success was my top priority, and I would work closely with him all year to ensure his success. Despite my efforts, after the first month he had a 37% and was well on his way to making his prediction a reality. After consulting with experienced teachers and researching other approaches,

I met with John and told him we would try something new. I told him I would not include any scores on assessments and instead would only include feedback on his responses. All I asked for in return was that John would be willing to meet with me after class to review the feedback and work together to build his skillset and his confidence. We would carefully review his responses, identify misconceptions, and identify prior knowledge to build on. As much as possible, he would take the lead on articulating his reasoning and clarifying his approach for a variety of concepts. He reluctantly accepted, and we got to work. He showed up to our sessions and quickly began to see success. Concepts that once seemed unattainable began to make sense, and he began to believe in his abilities. He started asking questions that probed deeper into the content and started to show a genuine interest in mathematics, especially as we applied them to real-world applications. In less than two months, John's desire to learn and engage with the content had been transformed. As the semester drew to a close, I met with him to show him his percentage in the course, which was based on his mastery: 87%. A tear of disbelief ran down his face as he had never received such a high mark in mathematics.

Other success stories based on formative data, actionable feedback, and differentiation come to mind whenever I reflect on the power of those after-school sessions. There was the student who used different color pencils to work through complex algebraic equations. And the student who drew visual diagrams using a massive scale on the whiteboard to make meaning. In a room full of students working with peer tutors to review concepts and formative assessments to identify mastery levels, the focus consistently remained on learning and not grades. Students understood that assessments were designed as checks for understanding and would be used to determine next steps, and they soon began to articulate their areas of strength and growth, a sure sign of their development as independent learners. That experience emphasized the impact developing students' growth mindset can have on achievement. In John's case, his success was built on formative data being used to drive learning. The focus on grades was replaced with a targeted effort to build capacity, and in the end, the grading took care of itself. How we use formative data and grading can dramatically impact our classroom culture and students' ability and willingness to tackle challenging tasks and better understand their own learning. From this process, John was able to articulate what he had mastered and what he was still working on: his language about his successes and opportunities had changed.

••

A growth mindset culture in your classroom cannot exist without formative data points because they are the evidence for students and teachers that progress toward mastery is being made and that targeted help to support that progress is readily available.

••

This shift in student thinking, however, cannot take place unless we also believe the same as educators. This means we must focus on learning, not scores, and give students multiple opportunities to demonstrate mastery. Students must believe that they can master content they have struggled with in the past, and that is only possible if they continuously focus on their learning and growth. The Researcher Dweck (2007) explains,

> Many teachers see evidence for a fixed mindset every year. The students who start out at the top of their class end up at the top, and the students who start out at the bottom end up there. Research by Falko Rheinberg shows that when teachers believe in fixed intelligence, this is exactly what happens. It is a self-fulfilling prophecy. However, when teachers hold a growth mindset, many students who start out lower in the class blossom during the year and join the higher achievers.   (p. 10)

Use Figure 2.1 to reflect on your own experience with growth mindset and how it can be an integral part of your instruction.

FIGURE 2.1 Your Own Experience With Growth Mindset

Think of your experience as a learner as you consider these prompts.	
Think of a time you grew as a learner by improving in an area you initially struggled in. What made you believe you could succeed?	
Did you have support and more than once chance to succeed?	
What long-term lessons did you take away from the experience?	

A growth mindset culture in your classroom cannot exist without formative data points because they are the evidence for students and teachers that progress toward mastery is being made and that targeted help to support that progress is readily available. If you intend to prioritize developing students' growth mindset as part of your classroom philosophy, a robust formative assessment approach must be part of your planning.

Formative Data Informs Instruction

We also briefly touched upon how instruction driven by formative data can impact student achievement. Each formative data point should lead to actionable next steps; otherwise, its impact is diminished. This means that your lessons will need to be flexible and may need adjustments on the fly or for the next day, depending on what the data show. With technology in the classroom, these adjustments can be made more quickly, frequently, and effectively to better meet the needs of all students. Jeong et al. (2020) explains, education must be assessment-focused and the cumulative capabilities of students must be established, together with providing opportunities for improvement . . . thus, online-based formative assessment interfaces have potential to be effectively integrated in educational situations as an appropriate tool for continuous and valuable interactions among instructors and learners. (p. 2)

For example, using technology to administer a short formative assessment can lead to immediate results, show which topics require additional support, and identify which students should be in which small group.

To make these next steps as actionable as possible, the questions included on the formative assessment must be carefully crafted to identify misconceptions and immediately lead to applicable supports. If you ask students to add ½ + ½, the answer choices should not be 1, 2, 3, and 4; instead, consider 1, 2/4, ¼ and other choices that will give you more information about student thinking. An incorrect answer should provide just as much information on next steps as the correct answer. Better yet, ask students to explain their next step ("Describe how you will add these two fractions"). Ask the type of questions that will lead to clear next steps. Analyzing the results takes moments, and the teacher can focus efforts on addressing them instead of breaking them down.

This integration of technology has been tremendously helpful in professional development settings as well as I learned during data analysis trainings with school site teams. Before adopting a technology-immersive approach, our meetings often started with sharing pertinent data points and starting a conversation about the implications derived from the results. Most of the hour-long meeting was consumed by exploring the data reports and discussing what they meant, resulting in only 10 or

15 minutes left for planning next steps to impact student learning. When we incorporated technology in a more intentional way, the outcome changed dramatically. Data was shared digitally, and collaborative documents were used to drive conversations, share findings, and offer a more individualized approach to planning next steps. Screencast videos using free programs like Screencastify or Screencast-o-matic were included to guide users through login information and data interpretation, offering additional technical support while moving the discussion forward. Soon, understanding the data took 10 to 15 minutes, leaving the majority of the session for planning actionable next steps. It took a few iterations to make this shift, but the result changed the way we use data points. Indeed, "the integration of instructional coaching with formative data serves as a promising approach for helping teachers enhance their use of universal practices" (Dudek et al., 2019, p. 91). We were not deterred by the learning curve required to bring about this change, and as we began to see the benefits, the transition accelerated.

•••

An incorrect answer should provide just as much information on next steps as the correct answer.

•••

Throughout the process, the focus stayed on actionable next steps to support learning, not the technology itself. Dalby and Swan (2019) explain, "the greatest challenge for teachers in using technology in the classroom is not the technology but an understanding of the process by which it can enhance student learning" (p. 843). Understanding how formative data can inform instruction was key throughout the process, and the more efficiently we are able to understand what the data points mean using technology, the more we can focus developing learning opportunities to address them.

CONNECTION TO COMPANION BOOK

Formative data points from classroom instruction and assessment are just one piece of the formative data analysis puzzle at the organizational level. The organizational level analysis includes attendance, graduation rate, socioemotional well-being, and other factors to create a more comprehensive view of the organization. Teacher input, however, must be an integral part in the analysis of many of these factors as they have tremendous insight into students' success indicators beyond academics. Teachers can witness students' socioemotional well-being and have conversations with students to better understand their attendance patterns. The companion book explores these other factors and how they can benefit from teacher input.

Formative Data Facilitates Differentiation and Promotes Equity

When discussing the impact of data on instructional planning, "a primary struggle . . . was understanding the difference between formative and summative data" (Beck et al., 2020, p. 158). While both provide helpful data to plan for future learning, formative data provides information to guide planning throughout the year, and summative provides a summary of students' learning at designated points in their learning. Schmid (2012) defines them well, stating, "Two main types of assessment, summative and formative, are typically referred to as *assessment of learning* and *assessment for learning*" (p. 75). The assessment *for* learning will ultimately lead to higher results on the assessment *of* learning; in other words, focusing on formative data will naturally result in stronger summative data outcomes. Prioritizing formative data over summative is also celebrated by students as they enjoy a focus on learning over grades, which is what education is about in the first place. Bibbens' (2018) research confirms that the [teachers and] the vast majority of students and parents . . . responded extremely positively to the shift to a systematic approach to formative assessment, both in its concept and in practice. It allowed a much-improved comparison of student work and therefore improved our ability to evaluate the efficacy of our practices. Taking an explicitly formative approach to assessment, one that highlighted growth and de-emphasised grades, initially led to more rigorous assessment of student work. This rigour did not lead to widespread discouragement as it had done in the past, but in fact encouraged collaboration between students and teacher. (p. 39)

The increased rigor facilitated by the focus on formative data is possible because the teacher gets consistent, actionable data to identify the supports needed for students to meet the expectations of the rigorous learning opportunities. Without these supports, deeper learning opportunities that push student thinking will be unattainable for some students, and these supports cannot be identified without formative data. Therefore, we can draw a straight line from effective formative data utilization to differentiated supports to access to more rigorous content for *all* students, confirming that formative data directly impacts equity in the classroom.

••

The assessment *for* learning will ultimately lead to higher results on the assessment *of* learning; in other words, focusing on formative data will naturally result in stronger summative data outcomes.

••

Employing rigorous learning opportunities with instructional technology also pushes students to research, critically evaluate findings, access supports, apply their own perspectives, and collaborate to reach mastery. Many low-rigor prompts can be addressed easily by students with an online search, offering even more incentive to generate learning activities that cannot simply be addressed with a quick Google search. This was a concern expressed repeatedly by teachers during distance learning as the sudden mass incorporation of technology impacted some learning prompts that were easily answered with access to the internet. In our conversations, we discussed that using technology to conduct research is an essential skill that we should incorporate into students' learning, and increasing the rigor through prompts that reflect higher levels of Bloom's Taxonomy will help them incorporate the benefits of technology in a meaningful way while enhancing their learning. As always, consistent, actionable formative data should be present to inform differentiated supports, both with and without technology, to move students toward mastery.

Schmid's (2012) research goes on to highlight the impact of formative data, explaining, "Research shows that an emphasis on assessment for learning significantly improves student performance (Black and William 1998). Therefore, greater reliance on formative assessment throughout K-12 education is recommended, especially in content areas that have cogent standards" (p. 75). Beck et al. (2020) acknowledge that internalizing this distinction can be challenging, explaining that

> even though participants [in the study] struggled with a nuanced understanding of formative and summative data, they clearly understood that formative data could be used to monitor student academic learning and evaluate their own teaching and saw this as the primary benefit of data. (p. 158)

Making this distinction is critical as formative data facilitates strategies for differentiated learning, while summative data assesses the effectiveness of those efforts. This impact on differentiation adds particular importance to the role of formative data even as the spotlight often shines more prominently on summative data due to the more formal nature of the results they represent.

••

We can draw a straight line from effective formative data utilization to differentiated supports to access to more rigorous content for *all* students, confirming that formative data directly impacts equity in the classroom.

••

Differentiating for students' needs is one of the most effective ways to celebrate and foster equity in your classroom. We know that students come from a wide variety of backgrounds and learn in different, multimodal ways, and we realize that meeting their needs requires a customized approach, not just one pace or approach for everyone. Despite our best efforts, we can usually differentiate for three levels at most: enrichment, intervention, and somewhere in the middle where we think most students are. Differentiating for every student with individualized supports is the ideal approach and one that meets the needs of every student, ultimately facilitating equity and access. This may seem well-meaning but ultimately unrealistic, but thanks to the dramatic increase in educators' expertise with instructional technology over recent years, it is closer than ever to becoming reality.

Technology can enhance formative data collection and application if prompts are designed to take advantage of its potential. Instructional technology can be used to present content through video, audio, and digital kinesthetic methods to make learning more accessible. Technology can also offer students a variety of ways to demonstrate mastery to better differentiate learning. To truly provide equitable access to learning, the formative assessments themselves can also be differentiated. In their studies, researchers highlight that educators:

understood the need to collect a variety of types of data to inform instruction to ensure that information being used to make instructional decisions was current and accurate. Participants indicated an understanding that this is particularly true for students from cognitively, culturally, and linguistically diverse backgrounds through their discourse regarding the alignment of the data collected and the decisions being made.

(Beck et al., 2020, p. 160)

Consider how technology can help students access content and share their understanding in ways not possible before. Take a text about the behavior of animals, for example. Instructional technology can dramatically increase access to the text in a variety of ways. Words that students may struggle with, such as the name of a particular species, can be hyperlinked to more information, increasing the text's accessibility for a variety of students. The link can show pictures of the animal, offer pronunciations of the name, present translation options for dozens of languages, and more. There can also be links to accept student responses and feedback in order to collect formative data that can inform instructional steps, small groups, and individualized supports. With instructional technology, the opportunities for rigorous and equitable access to learning is limitless.

•••

Differentiating for every student with individualized supports is the ideal approach and one that meets the needs of every student, ultimately facilitating equity and access.

•••

Use Figure 2.2 to reflect on how instructional technology and formative data can increase equitable access for all students. Before completing the prompt regarding equitable access in the final column, review your equity-focused classroom vision in Figure 1.2 from the previous chapter, and be sure your responses align to that vision. As we move into Part II, we will explore the possibilities in greater detail to maximize applicability in your classroom.

FIGURE 2.2 Incorporating Instructional Technology and Formative Data for Equity

Topic	Rigorous learning prompt	Formative data you would collect with technology	Differentiated supports you can provide based on the data	How this provides equitable access for all students

FORMATIVE DATA FOR SOCIAL JUSTICE

Individualized differentiation and an unrelenting focus on equity are critical elements of social justice; formative data can facilitate the use of both. Formative data informs planning and instruction to differentiate learning opportunities for students, often at an individualized level through the use of technology. Similarly, formative data promotes equity by providing information on students' strengths and areas of focus and ensuring that teachers have the information they need to equitably serve all students.

Key Takeaways

In this chapter, we examined the impact formative data can have on your instructional practice, particularly when its application is enhanced by technology. Specifically, we described how formative data fosters students' growth mindset by prioritizing learning over grades, offers differentiated supports and multiple opportunities to demonstrate mastery, informs differentiated supports to meet the needs of students (especially when technology is incorporated to offer supports specific to *each* student), and promotes equity by offering a variety of ways for students to access content. In Part II, we will build on these takeaways to develop practical next steps and bring your equity-focused classroom vision to life.

Part II
Effective Formative Data Use in the New Classroom

3
Maximizing the Effectiveness of Formative Data

Part I: The Need to Reevaluate How We Use Data in the Classroom

Changing Instructional Data Considerations Due to ... (*Introduction*)
♦ Advancements in Technology Changing Formative Data Use
♦ Loss of Consistent Summative Data From Previous Academic Years
♦ Concerns About Data Reliability Due to Increased Remote Assessment
♦ Concerns About "Learning Loss" During Distance Learning

NECESSITATE NEED TO REVISIT VISION

Your Classroom's Vision and Beliefs (*Chapter 1*)
♦ Assessing Your Classroom Vision
♦ Reflecting on Your Beliefs About Student Learning and Your Role
♦ Where Formative Data Fits In

WHICH GUIDE FORMATIVE DATA ROLE AND ITS IMPACT

The Impact of Formative Data on Student Success (*Chapter 2*)
♦ Formative Data Fosters Students' Growth Mindset
♦ Formative Data Informs Instruction
♦ Formative Data Facilitates Differentiation and Promotes Equity

DOI: 10.4324/9781003246213-6

Part II: Effective Formative Data Use in the New Classroom

Maximizing the Effectiveness of Formative Data (Chapter 3)	Using Instructional Technology to Effectively Address Formative Data (Chapter 4)	Building Student Capacity Through Formative Data (Chapter 5)	Analyzing Formative Data Collaboratively to Identify and Celebrate Best Practices (Chapter 6)
♦ How *Actionable* Is the Data You Are Gathering? ♦ How *Timely* Is the Data You Are Gathering? ♦ How Much Data Do You Need?	♦ On-the-Fly Formative Data for Whole Class Instruction ♦ Formative Assessments for Differentiated Learning	♦ Digital Self-Assessment Rubrics ♦ Self-Selected Small Groups ♦ Self-Monitored Digital Success Trackers	♦ PLCs ♦ Peer Observations—In-Person and Virtual ♦ Teacher-Led Professional Development ♦ Success Celebration Events

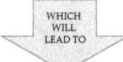

Innovative Learning in the New Classroom *(Chapter 7)*
♦ Re-envisioning Learning for All Students
♦ Reflecting on the Focus on Summative and Formative Assessments
♦ Preparing Students to Be Lifelong Independent Learners

In Part I, we examined how the changing educational landscape driven by the distance learning experience has created an opportunity for us to incorporate instructional technology into classrooms to enhance learning. We reviewed the power of a classroom vision that utilizes technology and formative data to offer equitable and personalized access to learning and explored some of the many benefits that formative data points offer to bring the vision to life. Adopting an equity-focused vision backed by a sincere desire to serve all students and coupled with a commitment to differentiate using formative data is the first big step in transforming learning, but it is not the last. In our data-rich world, it can be challenging to identify which data points will impact student achievement the most and to avoid the dreaded "analysis paralysis." As I shared from my experience working with school teams in the Introduction, priority must be given to data that is directly connected to next steps that support student learning. We must have a sense of urgency about our work because our students, especially those who are at-risk, do not have the luxury of waiting long for our data analysis. Every assessment we present to students is time taken from learning opportunities and must therefore inform our instruction and planning in order to be worthwhile. For this reason, all formative data points we collect must be actionable, timely, and just the right amount for us to identify next steps. This approach supports a "lean" approach to formative assessment, one that uses it only when it will be immediately applicable and only with enough prompts to provide the information necessary to inform next steps. Take this approach seriously to maximize instructional time; if you only intend to look at two prompts, don't include three. It may not seem like a sizeable difference, but over the course of a year and over a hundred formative assessments, it will add up to an incredible amount of instructional time.

Remember that focusing on actionable next steps ties assessments directly to instruction; if you determine that an assessment is taking away from instruction, that assessment is not being used to inform instruction.

Formative data collection and application must occur regularly in the classroom, though Anderson et al. (2010) explain,

> Data use in schools is largely a collective activity involving principals with teachers in multiple contexts (e.g., school improvement teams, grade or subject team meetings, at-risk student committee meetings, faculty meetings). Principals often act more as enablers of data use by teachers (e.g., providing access to data, tools, time, and expertise, and holding teachers accountable for data use), than as data users themselves. (p. 319)

If we wait for occasional data meetings as the only time we closely look at data, the results will be limited in their actionability and timeliness. Hattie (2012) explains,

> The aim is to provide feedback that is "just in time", "just for me", "just for where I am in my learning process" and "just what I need to help me move forward". There is a need to be aware that such feedback can come from many sources (and that such feedback can't be wrong!). (p. 122)

These three elements for feedback ensure that it is timely and differentiated to meet the specific needs of each student. In this chapter, we will examine how to identify these types of formative data points and how to utilize instructional technology to make capturing them as efficient as possible to maximize instruction.

How *Actionable* Is the Data You Are Gathering?

Identifying actionable data is not always as straightforward as it sounds. Any data point can lead to conclusions that suggest next steps for action, but those action steps may be related more closely to reporting instead of immediately impacting student achievement. Jorno and Gynther (2018) explain that "[actionable] . . . indicates that analytics is concerned with the potential for practical action rather than either theoretical description or mere reporting" (p. 202). Actionable formative data are critical for creating the differentiated learning opportunities we discussed in previous chapters that foster equity and access, which means we must be very intentional about planning how our formative data will be used. There are several characteristics that actionable data points typically share; once we identify them, we can better plan on how we will collect and use them. Remember that focusing on actionable next steps ties assessments directly to instruction; if you determine that an assessment is taking away from instruction, that assessment is not being used to inform instruction.

IMPLEMENTATION TIP

How will you determine what formative data points are actionable? Keep in mind that collecting formative data that is only informative may take away from instructional time without providing data to further support students. As you design prompts, consider how you will use the results during the same lesson or within a couple of days depending on the scope of the assessment. You should be able to articulate your next step with the data points and be satisfied with it before you present the prompt to your students.

Actionable Data Is Easily Accessible

Truly actionable data are easily accessible; if the data points are challenging to collect, some of the effort required to access them will inevitably impact the likelihood of regular collection and utilization. Time and effort are limited resources, so we must design our formative data plan to impact both as little as possible. Utilizing instructional technology can assist with this, especially when using prompts and assessments that are automatically evaluated and presented in grouped outcomes. For example, the results of a short formative assessment developed with the quiz function of the Google Forms app can easily be exported into Google Sheets, which offers filtering options to assist with identifying students for small group instruction based on the results. The entire process can take just a few minutes and offer immediate next steps through grouping. It is also important to consider the type of questions you will include and what they will tell you about student learning. If you develop a plan for next steps for each question before administering the formative assessment, you will become more critical of the questions you include. This in turn will keep your formative assessments short, reducing the amount of time taken from instruction. Each and every question should lead to actionable next steps. Reflect on a recent formative assessment you administered and what actions resulted from each question using Figure 3.1. As you answer the prompts, consider how the questions were accessible for all students and how you differentiated learning based on your findings.

FIGURE 3.1 Reflecting on Your Formative Assessments

List some of the questions from the formative assessment here	Explain how you accessed the results	How long did it take?	What next steps did you take with the results?

A helpful strategy to assist with making formative data easily accessible is by systematizing how you collect and access the data points. If you are able to continue to offer a variety of formative assessments, consider using a limited number of apps to gather the data points. If you will need multiple apps to collect and analyze the data points, find a way to consolidate them in one place. Nyland (2018) states, "We should place more effort on developing customizable instructor dashboards that present a variety of choices for displaying student data" (p. 522). One way to accomplish this with limited effort is to use a website or a Google Docs page that includes links to all of the apps in one page. Links and steps for accessing the data can be included as well. The more you can organize the data and simplify your analysis process, the more likely you will regularly access the site and use the data points. Having the data points in one place can also facilitate identifying trends and patterns that can inform planning. Using Figure 3.2, make an inventory of the apps or strategies you currently use to gather and utilize formative data points. Use your notes to summarize your formative data collection and use approach and to determine your system's level of actionability.

FIGURE 3.2 Reflecting on Your Formative Data System

List apps/ strategies you currently use to collect formative data	Describe how you use the results	Share how effective this approach is compared to others	Can this approach be updated in any way to make its use more effective?
Based on your notes above, summarize your formative data collection and use approach and determine your system's level of actionability.			

Actionable Data Can Be Understood by Students

Formative data is more actionable when it can be understood by students as students take a more active role in next steps identified. From their research, Cakir et al. (2016) conclude, "More than half of the students frequently preferred formative feedback that is useful" (p. 26). Helping students understand formative data points dramatically impacts the development of their growth mindset as they become active participants in their learning (refer back to the previous chapter for more information on the connection between formative data and growth mindset). This access to formative data also fosters students' growth as independent learners as they take more ownership of their learning, a critical element in promoting equity in education.

••

If you develop a plan for next steps for each question before administering the formative assessment, you will become more critical of the questions you include. This in turn will keep your formative assessments short, reducing the amount of time taken from instruction.

••

Students' awareness of their own learning and their ability to self-assess do not occur on their own, especially if they have not had exposure to these ideas before; they must be trained to understand actionable data. Generally, these skills are reinforced in more affluent school communities compared to many schools in low socioeconomic areas, which traditionally have a more teacher-driven approach. Building student capacity to understand formative data, then, can have a direct impact on closing the achievement gap. Teachers can build student expertise with understanding their own learning by:

- Establishing that in your classroom, every topic is either mastered or yet-to-be-mastered. Data will show progress and progress never ceases.
- Articulating clear objectives for each lesson and how mastery will be measured.
- Training students on how to identify their areas of strength and how to articulate what they are working on at the moment.
- Teaching students how to self-identify areas of focus and access differentiated support for those areas. For example, students can understand that they should join a small group to review a particular topic if they struggled with a specific question on the formative assessment.
- Exposing students to data regularly and training them on how to read data points.

The recommendation in the previous section to house links to all formative data apps in one place can serve to assist access to students. You can record screencasts to show how to access and understand results and link them to the same site or page. For apps that students log into to access their data, you can include login information, screencasts for support, and next steps. Class-wide data can also be displayed to facilitate conversations with students about the results, which can be a great first step to implementing actionable supports. Nicholson et al. (2017) concludes, "Learning to position students' thinking and understanding as central pillars of teaching practice is another foundation underlying productive data conversations" (p. 187). Like data analysis discussions with colleagues, conversations with students should be planned from the outset to lead to next steps.

To make the conversations meaningful, consider the data points that will provide the most actionable next steps. At times, the data points we are accustomed to working with are not the ones that inform next steps. Scale scores, for example, often do not provide actionable next steps even though they are among the more popular data points produced by assessments. A raw score such as 150 or 2230 does not give meaningful feedback to act on and only serves to show relative performance compared to other students. Data on specific standards and skills offer more information about student mastery levels. This approach creates opportunities for gathering details that can provide valuable insight that may be excluded from overall scores. Incorrect or inadequate responses revealed from looking closely at skills or standards may offer more about student understanding than the correct answer, leading to more targeted actionable next steps. A common misconception identified in the responses by a small number of students on a formative assessment can lead to clear next steps in a small group to address their misunderstanding.

Using language that students understand and sharing detailed formative assessment outcomes with them can help students better understand content and, perhaps more importantly, better understand their own understanding. Having a clear vision for what we want students to know is critical in designing formative assessments that inform our next steps. Finnegan et al. (2019) explain,

> Educators should design instruction with a learning goal in mind and must ask themselves the critical question of, "What do I want students to know, understand, and be able to do?" (Tomlinson, 2017). This is designing for understanding; one of the basic tenets of designing for understanding occurs when students can autonomously make sense of and transfer their learning through some facet of authentic performance through explanation, interpretation, application, alteration in their perspective, empathy, or self-assessment of knowledge. (p. 3)

As students develop metacognition around their own learning, they will become skilled at using formative data to identify their strengths and their areas of growth and be better equipped to address them.

Consider Schmid's (2012, p. 81) seven Assessment Maxims as a guide to inform assessment planning:

1. All assessments must be driven by what students need to know. The question of how to determine which students understand the concept or skill and which students need intervention must be determined at the onset.
2. Formative assessments inform the teacher about the learner and the learner about himself or herself. Summative assessments that are valid and reliable provide programmatic information about content coverage and overall achievement.

3. Raw data alone do not provide sufficient evidence of learning to form the basis of evaluation regarding students' proficiencies. Information gleaned from data that provides good evidence of learning empowers teachers and students to engage in intentional teaching and learning cycles.
4. Research indicates formative assessment helps struggling students take greater ownership of their own progress toward learning targets, thereby enabling them to learn more quickly.
5. It is incumbent on teachers to design and implement assessments that enable the stakeholders to gain insight into what students know and can do.
6. Teachers and students must understand their strengths, weaknesses, proficiencies, proclivities, and aptitudes to access these attributes, remediate gaps in motor skill development, and accommodate the abilities of the learner. Literacy and fluency . . . require declarative and procedural knowledge, necessitating the use of varied methodologies for gathering evidence of learning.
7. Good record keeping is essential to effective measurement of student proficiencies to map growth over time.

Notice how they repeatedly emphasize that formative data is accessed and understood by both teacher *and* students, particularly in items 2–6. This is the philosophy we must adopt to maximize the utility of formative assessments; making formative data accessible and understandable to students greatly increases their applicability as well as student's development as independent learners. This access, however, cannot exist without careful planning by the teacher. A clear plan must be in place for how students can access and interpret formative data results. Using Figure 3.3, identify how you can make formative data accessible to students to maximize their impact.

FIGURE 3.3 How Students Access Formative Assessments

Type of Formative Assessment	How Students Can Access Results	What Action Steps You Expect Them to Take	Desired Outcome

Actionable Data Utilizes Instructional Technology to Maximize Differentiation

With the influx of instructional technology made available in recent years, we have an opportunity to differentiate at an individual level based on formative data. Access to technology is not enough, as Dalby and Swan (2019) observe: "the pertinent question to ask is not whether digital technology is being used but how its usage supports teaching and learning" (p. 833). Technology can lead to increased differentiation and therefore more robust actionable next steps in several ways. First, it can automatically export results to a spreadsheet to allow for sorting and filtering to inform grouping, facilitating student supports based on the data. Second, it can be used to "push" supports or next steps to students based on the formative data. For example, students who demonstrate a misconception can be sent a mini-lesson that offers clarification and another opportunity to demonstrate mastery. Third, technology can be used to facilitate student self-monitoring and choice, critical elements of building students' capacity as independent learners. Based on the outcomes of formative assessments, students can choose from a variety of next steps on your class website, such as enrichment activities, deeper exploration into different topics related to the lesson, and additional supports. They can also choose from different learning projects that cater to their interests and current mastery levels, critical opportunities that foster equity in your classroom. The opportunities are limitless.

Your classroom culture must be designed to facilitate this type of learning. Establishing a community in which students understand that everyone is working toward the same objectives but may be in different places on the journey, and creating an expectation that all students demonstrate respect for each other and the learning process, is key. Directions for next steps must also be shared, and the processes for rotating to different groups and sharing progress must be practiced in order for the teacher to serve as a facilitator. Students must know when they are ready for the next step of the learning process and where to get help. This can be quite different from what they are used to and requires training and practice as well as a clear understanding of their new role as independent learners.

Think of a cross-country trip from Los Angeles to New York with students following you in their own cars (this analogy appears in the companion book in a different context—use it or your preferred analogy to help move your team's thinking). You need to arrive in New York with all students, so you will need to check in your rearview mirror often to make sure they are all still following you; these checks are your formative data points. Checking the rearview mirror is not enough, however; if someone is missing, you will need to take action to get them back on the road. Equity comes into consideration when different students need different supports. One student may be out of gas, while another may have a flat tire, and yet another may have taken a wrong exit. You'll need to provide differentiated supports—a canister full of gas, a new tire, a navigation system—to make sure each student gets back on the road. Students will need to understand that each of them may need something different to stay on the road; your differentiated assistance will ensure everyone is successful.

How *Timely* Is the Data You Are Gathering?

Formative data points can transform learning when they are actionable, but timing also plays a critical role in their effectiveness. Actionable next steps can lose their potency if they take too much time to implement. Student learning must consistently be assessed to inform instruction and planning, and taking too much time to provide feedback and offer next steps can be detrimental to their growth. Chung et al. (2006) explain,

> The most effective form of assessment is one that is continuous, that occurs as close as possible to the scene of the action in teaching and learning (the classroom), and that provides diagnostic feedback to both teachers and students—to teachers on how they can improve their teaching, to students on how they can improve their learning. (p. 19)

The emphasis on limiting the gap between the formative assessment and the ensuing next steps plays a dramatic role in the effectiveness of the data gleaned from the assessment.

Technology can help accelerate formative data sharing and facilitate next steps if carefully designed before the lesson. Robertson et al. (2019) explains,

> While technology is often used to connect students to resources, it can also be used to support formative assessment. The challenges that can derive from determining the effectiveness of formative assessments can arise from how and when the formative assessments are provided. For example, Bhagat and Spector (2017) found that if feedback is delayed, it may not support student learning or engagement and that constructive feedback could be perceived the wrong way and have a negative impact on

the learning process. Consequently, immediacy was one of the biggest instructors and student benefits of using the technology tool. (p. 2)

As mentioned earlier in this chapter, limiting the number of prompts in each formative assessment can help make the results more actionable as well as timelier. Extensive formative assessments can take time to process in addition to offering too much information to take action on at that moment; adopt a philosophy with frequent, shorter formative assessments to maintain actionability and timeliness.

CONNECTION TO COMPANION BOOK

The meaning of "timely" may differ between data at the organizational level and in the classroom. Formative data points in the classroom should be used to address misconceptions or inform small group planning either the same day or by the next lesson. In contrast, formative data at the organizational level is not addressed within days; rather, it is reviewed and discussed during regularly recurring planning meetings.

How Soon Will You Be Able to Act On the Data?

As you develop your formative assessments, you should be keenly aware of when you will access the results and when you will apply them to your instructional plan. We know that

instructional technology can play a key role in analyzing the responses to a formative assessment and providing feedback quickly to students to maintain progress toward mastery. Where a short formative assessment on paper can take time to score and consolidate, the one using technology can generate individual and class data to

> inform next steps in a timely manner. Getting feedback to students shortly after the formative assessment dramatically increases the impact of the assessment as the data inform additional supports and review needed before progressing further. (Mekhitarian, 2021, p. 74)

Administering formative assessments without a clear plan of action will inevitably lead to inconsistent actionable next steps, resulting in the assessment not serving its intended purpose and ultimately taking time away from instruction without direct benefit to the learning process. Ideally, formative assessments will lead to action that same day, and in some cases, the next day. If you will not be able to utilize the data in that time frame, reconsider administering it and review it to see if it needs to be trimmed down further to facilitate implementation and easy applicability.

TECH TIP

More robust formative assessments can offer an array of data points to inform next steps, such as how small groups should be created and what misconceptions need to be addressed. Identifying these takeaways can take time, a luxury that can limit the impact of the findings. To minimize the time between the formative assessment and the implementation of the next steps based on the findings, try to use an assessment platform that automatically collects the results and facilitates efficient analysis. Programs that can export results to Excel, for example, have an advantage because Excel offers easy filtering, sorting, and grouping. Using a cloud version of a spreadsheet such as Google Sheets can facilitate collaborative data review and analysis with other colleagues, especially when co-teaching. Use technology to expedite the process of identifying *what* to focus on so more time can be devoted to *how* to address it.

How Much Data Do You Need?

Determining the proper length of formative assessments cannot be overemphasized. But what is the proper length? There is no correct number of prompts or a recommended time duration; instead, the best practice is to include just enough in the formative assessment to give you only data you will be able to use right away. The most important factor in determining this is your plan for actionable next steps based on the data points. If you plan to create rotating small groups to review different prompts based on the formative assessment results, for example, consider the prompts needed to implement that activity.

More extensive formative assessments that offer a deeper exploration of student mastery can lead to actionable next steps the next day. With technology, however, you do not need to wait until the next class session to share the results and next steps, especially if you are on a block schedule in which classes do not meet every day. You can share results remotely and ask students to explore resources associated with them before the next class session. This of course will require training, practice, and a positive classroom culture that reinforces accountability through a caring lens. The formative learning process is now a continuous one that can continue between class periods through the use of instructional technology.

FORMATIVE DATA FOR SOCIAL JUSTICE

Assessment time takes away from instruction, which all students—especially at-risk students—need to be successful. Therefore, any time taken for formative assessments must have actionable takeaways to enhance instruction. Choose your formative assessments carefully and only include prompts on which you are prepared to act upon. Gathering more data points than you will be able to address in a timely manner can have negative consequences because that time could have gone to instruction and support.

How Much Time Will It Take to Collect the Data, and Will You Be Able to Address All the Data You Collect?

Finally, consider how much time it will take to collect the data. Each minute of data collection is time taken from other learning opportunities, so we develop efficient ways to gather formative data. There must be a sense of urgency around our work in the classroom to maximize learning. Use technology to design and distribute formative assessments and to collect formative data. Some of the apps described in Chapter 3—Google Forms, Kahoot, and Nearpod—can all offer rapid formative assessment distribution, but you can also consider other sites to gather more open-ended formative data. Google Jamboard and AnswerGarden both offer ways to collect student responses and view them easily as well. Jamboard allows students to post responses under different banners and visualize connections between responses using a variety of tools, while AnswerGarden magnifies the size of the most common responses to quickly identify trends and patterns in student thinking. Choosing the correct program should be based on what you intend to do with the data and how it will inform instruction. As in any profession, you need the right tool for the job at hand.

Key Takeaways

In this chapter, we explored the best practices to consider as you develop your formative assessments, particularly their actionability and timeliness. We also discussed how to determine the most appropriate amount of data to gather in each formative assessment to inform planning without taking too much time away from instruction. In the next chapter, we will connect these ideas to implementation through technology, focusing heavily on the potential impact of formative data on personalized differentiation.

4

Using Instructional Technology to Effectively Address Formative Data

Part I: The Need to Reevaluate How We Use Data in the Classroom

Changing Instructional Data Considerations Due to . . . (*Introduction*)
♦ Advancements in Technology Changing Formative Data Use
♦ Loss of Consistent Summative Data From Previous Academic Years
♦ Concerns About Data Reliability Due to Increased Remote Assessment
♦ Concerns About "Learning Loss" During Distance Learning

Your Classroom's Vision and Beliefs (*Chapter 1*)
♦ Assessing Your Classroom Vision
♦ Reflecting on Your Beliefs About Student Learning and Your Role
♦ Where Formative Data Fits In

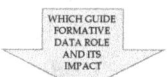

The Impact of Formative Data on Student Success (*Chapter 2*)
♦ Formative Data Fosters Students' Growth Mindset
♦ Formative Data Informs Instruction
♦ Formative Data Facilitates Differentiation and Promotes Equity

DOI: 10.4324/9781003246213-7

Part II: Effective Formative Data Use in the New Classroom

Maximizing the Effectiveness of Formative Data *(Chapter 3)*	Using Instructional Technology to Effectively Address Formative Data *(Chapter 4)*	Building Student Capacity Through Formative Data *(Chapter 5)*	Analyzing Formative Data Collaboratively to Identify and Celebrate Best Practices *(Chapter 6)*
♦ How *Actionable* Is the Data You Are Gathering? ♦ How *Timely* Is the Data You Are Gathering? ♦ How Much Data Do You Need?	♦ On-the-Fly Formative Data for Whole Class Instruction ♦ Formative Assessments for Differentiated Learning	♦ Digital Self-Assessment Rubrics ♦ Self-Selected Small Groups ♦ Self-Monitored Digital Success Trackers	♦ PLCs ♦ Peer Observations—In-Person and Virtual ♦ Teacher-Led Professional Development ♦ Success Celebration Events

Innovative Learning in the New Classroom *(Chapter 7)*
♦ Re-envisioning Learning for All Students ♦ Reflecting on the Focus on Summative and Formative Assessments ♦ Preparing Students to Be Lifelong Independent Learners

In the previous chapter, we explored the characteristics of formative data points that would be actionable and timely; we must now review the logistical considerations to make gathering them on a regular basis efficient and manageable. In this chapter, we will explore two types of formative assessments—on-the-fly and pre-planned—and how they can inform instruction and differentiation. Both types of formative assessments impact classroom pedagogy but often result in varying actionable next steps.

Regardless of the type of formative assessment employed, asking thoughtful questions that reveal critical insights into students' understanding is essential. In *Development of Formative Assessment Tool for a Primary, Technology Classroom*, researchers explain,

> There is increasing understanding in literature and classrooms that questions should be the starting point of a dialogue. The purpose of these dialogues in the classroom

could be for teaching, learning or assessment, especially formative assessment. Formative assessment carried out in the interaction between teacher and students could assist the teacher in deciding the direction of learning for the students. Formative assessment is linked to substantial learning gains. (RR et al., 2020, p. 101)

We will explore best practices for using instructional technology in on-the-fly and planned formative assessments to inform learning with thoughtful questioning.

FORMATIVE DATA FOR SOCIAL JUSTICE

Using instructional technology for formative assessment can provide easily actionable data with instant results, clear visualizations, and other helpful features, but care must be taken to ensure equity and access for all students. Limited access to instructional technology can hamper students' ability to provide feedback critical for their learning; be sure all students have equal access to resources to provide formative data before proceeding.

On-the-Fly Formative Data for Whole Class Instruction

When considering how to use formative data in the classroom, it is important to reflect on how it will be gathered and what steps are needed to prepare. Some formative assessments—especially those requiring instructional technology—involve planning in advance, while others can be done on-the-fly based on the progression of the lesson. A formative quiz, for example, needs to be developed in advance to ensure it includes thoughtful questions and does not require instructional time to create. Because these planned assessments are created outside of the classroom, the teacher can take time to incorporate detailed questions that can inform differentiation, small group instruction, and interventions to ensure all students are successful. On-the-fly formative assessments, on the other hand, are developed on the spot, take just a few moments to administer, and provide broader formative feedback to gauge understanding. Both types of formative assessments are important even though there is a clear tradeoff: on-the-fly formative assessments are quickly administered on the spot but provide less detail, while planned formative assessments take time to create but can offer individualized data. As Schmid (2012) notes, "teachers must employ multiple measures to gather evidence of learning over time" (p. 76).

On-the-fly questions can provide a variety of formative data to inform instruction, but not all questions need to check for understanding. Some may give you information about student interests, which may impact how you proceed with a lesson. Since these questions only take a moment to pose, they can be helpful in engaging students while taking minimal instructional time. For example, if you are going to teach a lesson on fractions using a recipe, you may consider a prompt that asks them to pick one of four recipes. While the question does not provide insight into student understanding, it does provide information on student interests, which can engage students. The opportunity to provide feedback on the recipe helps students connect to the content, and the feedback gathered can be used in one of two ways:

- To inform whole class instruction.
- To allow students to self-select differentiated groups or activities based on their responses.

CONNECTION TO COMPANION BOOK

The nature of organizational formative data analysis requires regularly scheduled meetings and data collected over a period of time to present for analysis. As such, all formative data points reviewed at the organizational level are generated from pre-planned activities; no on-the-fly data gathering is involved. Administering on-the-fly formative assessments as needed is strictly a challenge for teachers who need real-time information to make instructional decisions in a moment's notice.

••

Polling

Polling programs are among the most efficient ways to gather on-the-fly formative data. They allow teachers to quickly gather feedback from students without the need for login information or other steps to get started. Poll questions are easy to develop on the spot if needed, but their simplified nature limits applications for individualized differentiation. A variety of resources can be used to quickly gather feedback from students, including polling in Zoom, polling using physical clickers, and polling added directly in presentations. In each case, the teacher decides to administer a poll based on the progress of the lesson and the potential need to review content with some or all of the class. Most formative assessments are pre-planned and built into the lesson with clear next steps design in advance; on-the-fly formative assessments such as polls developed mid-lesson come about when the teacher needs more information on student understanding at that moment than originally planned. In these instances, a quick poll can provide the feedback necessary to determine how to proceed with the lesson.

••

On-the-fly formative assessments have their place in the classroom because lessons do not always go as planned and being flexible and data-driven can yield greater student achievement. However, more detailed formative assessments must also be integrated into every lesson design with clear, actionable next steps planned for the results.

••

Keyword Programs

Another on-the-fly formative data tool is a keyword program like AnswerGarden, which allows students to respond to a prompt or question with a brief answer. The answers submitted are added to a growing word graphic with more popular responses being displayed in larger font. Ultimately, a collage of answers appears for the entire class to see, and the most frequently occurring responses are easily identifiable by their size. Note that the collage works best if the question posed elicits one-word or one-phrase responses so that duplicated answers can be recorded. Asking "why" or "how" questions will result in many unique responses and may not reveal themes in the responses. Once again, the keyword-type, on-the-fly assessments provide limited detail for individualized differentiation but can be added to a lesson quickly if more information is needed.

Quick Surveys

Teachers can also make a quick one- or two-question Google Forms survey to gather on-the-fly formative data. One advantage of Google Forms over the other options is the ability to choose from a variety of question types, including checkbox questions that accept more than one answer. A one-question survey does not take very long to make on the spot, and pushing out the survey is easy with a shortened link or a pushout through Google Classroom. Use Figure 4.1 to reflect on how these on-the-fly formative assessment approaches can inform your instruction.

FIGURE 4.1 On-the-Fly Formative Assessment

On-the-Fly Formative Assessment	Which part of your lesson might this impact?	How will you use the data gathered to inform next steps?
Polling		
Keyword		
Quick Surveys		

Formative Assessments for Differentiated Learning

On-the-fly formative assessments have their place in the classroom because lessons do not always go as planned, and being flexible and data-driven can yield greater student achievement. However, more detailed formative assessments must also be integrated into every lesson design with clear, actionable next steps planned for the results. Instructional technology can serve to gather formative data and quickly address it. In addition to informing whole class instruction, formative assessments can provide insight into differentiated grouping and individualized supports. Groups can be determined by the teacher based on results or through student self-selection. For example, students can be asked to join one of several groups based on their responses or can even choose which group to join based on what needed supports they self-identify. This is, of course, an advanced skill we must train our students to master, but one that is critical for building growth mindset and self-monitoring. We will discuss self-monitoring strategies with digital resources in more detail in the next chapter. QR codes, or 'quick response' codes, can be used to provide instructions for next steps for each group. These two-dimensional versions of barcodes can be scanned to produce more content and can be placed around the room for students to access. This adds a layer of engagement while simultaneously making each grouping feel different—not better or worse—than each other since students are not going to groups that "got it right" or "got it wrong." QR codes can be generated quickly and without charge on a variety of sites.

Common Formative Assessments Generated Through Instructional Technology

Several programs facilitate the development and implementation of formative assessments and provide detailed results breakdowns to expedite analysis and data-driven decision-making.

When choosing a program to support this process, consider the data analysis efficiency, among other factors. As the companion book *Harnessing Formative Data for K-12 Leaders* states, if the finite amount of time and energy we have goes to gathering the data, little of each will be left for analysis and planning actionable next steps. One particularly strong assessment program is Illuminate. In addition to facilitating the development of formative assessments with questions developed from the teacher that can be typed or hand-written, Illuminate offers massive question banks that can be used to create formative assessments based on topics or standards chosen.

Teachers can also grant access to the formative assessment in Illuminate to their colleagues, allowing collaborative assessment development and administration. This process produces *common* formative assessments that can greatly impact the analysis of the results. For example, if two teachers administer the same common formative assessment, and students in one classroom demonstrate higher mastery for a particular topic assessed, the teachers can discuss this finding in the debrief, and the teacher can share how he/she approached the topic to get strong results from the students. The other teacher now has a potential, actionable next step to consider. As an additional benefit, common formative assessments also facilitate co-planning of lessons, which can build pedagogical expertise.

As you choose your formative assessment platform, consider programs that will help you identify misconceptions quickly. For multiple choice questions, programs can offer this feature by showing the percentage at which each answer choice was selected instead of just the percentage of students who chose the correct answer. If 30% of students chose correct answer A in this example but we see that 55% of students gravitated toward answer choice D, we can reasonably suspect that a misconception shared by more than half the students led them to that answer. Reviewing the answers for A and D can reveal the misconception and give teachers the formative data they need to plan next steps.

Answer Choice	A (correct)	B	C	D
Percentage Chosen by Students	30%	10%	5%	55%

Formative data points on misconceptions provide even more detail on student understanding than information on whether students answered correctly; misconceptions uncover insights into student thinking and can potentially lead to deeper discussions and greater learning opportunities.

Based on the formative assessment results, you can determine which standards or questions require small group intervention and which require whole group review. If smaller percentages of students did not demonstrate mastery, small group intervention may be the best approach. However, consider how you will move from the formative assessment to small groups without creating stigma around being pulled into a small group for not having demonstrated mastery. How you label groups will also play a role in students' comfort level with small group instruction. No one wants to be singled out for remediation, and framing small groups as opportunities to explore a concept further can increase student readiness to engage in small groups. Students must also understand that small groups are part of our focus on equity, meaning not all students will receive identical supports in order to be successful. Some students may be coming from educational experiences that only included whole group instruction, so differentiated small groups may take some getting used to. They must understand your intention and trust you. Figure 4.2 shows one sequence you can follow to address formative data that provides differentiated supports for all students and includes prompts to facilitate reflection on each step.

In this sequence, the teacher reviews formative data in the class and has determined how groupings will be set up as part of the lesson. When using common formative assessments, be sure to create time between lessons whenever possible to collaboratively review results and share best practices.

FIGURE 4.2 Formative Assessment Sequence Example

Part of Sequence	Instructional Technology Use	Question to Consider	Your Response
Teacher introduces lesson through direct instruction.	Lesson can be recorded for future viewing, including review in small groups.	How will on-the-fly formative assessments inform instruction on the way to the planned formative assessment?	
Teacher uses formative assessment to measure student understanding.	A variety of programs can be used, including Illuminate and Google Forms.	How will you determine which questions will give you enough information for actionable next steps without taking too much time?	
Teacher reviews formative data, including any insights on student misconceptions.	Ensure the program used offers clear and easy-to-analyze results.	Which program will present formative data in a format that facilitates quick analysis?	
Teacher creates groups for differentiated work.	Prompts for each group can be made available on the teacher site or can be assigned with QR codes at the physical group spaces.	How will you create differentiated groups for independent practice, enrichment, and collaboration that build on the lesson?	
Students work in differentiated groups while teacher pulls small groups to review content based on formative data.	Formative assessment programs can be used to check for understanding in smaller groups as well.	How will you create a classroom culture that accepts that some students need additional support based on formative assessment data?	
Teacher continues to next lesson that builds on previous learning.	A visualization can show how the lessons connect to establish and build on context.	What evidence will demonstrate that the class is ready to proceed?	

Formative Assessments Built Into Lesson Presentations

Formative assessments can also be built directly into lessons when using presentation-style programs like Nearpod or Poll Everywhere. As you develop your presentation, you can insert formative assessment questions directly into the lesson to pause and check for understanding. While this approach makes the learning process more linear, it does ensure thoughtful questioning at pivotal moments to catch misconceptions early on before proceeding. In Nearpod, teachers can create interactive lessons that move through various information screens and questions in sync as a class; when the teacher moves to the next slide, so do all students at the same time. Formative assessments built in this way engage students, give teachers immediate feedback on mastery, and allow for pre-planning to develop thoughtful prompts. Poll Everywhere works similarly but is designed as an add-on to PowerPoint. Like Nearpod, Poll Everywhere makes a lesson interactive but does so by incorporating formative assessment questions into PowerPoint. The questions can be answered by students using a mobile device.

These tools are far more advanced than the clickers I used for formative assessments in the classroom many years ago, but they serve a similar purpose. I incorporated carefully designed formative questions in my presentations, and students would use physical clickers to select a response. Answer choices included several responses designed to surface misconceptions so I could quickly find and address them. I also incorporated on-the-fly formative assessments as needed, sometimes by simply writing a few choices on the whiteboard and asking students to use their clickers to select one. Most importantly, each and every formative prompt was designed to inform an actionable next step; if time from instruction is to be taken for an assessment, that assessment must be in the service of instruction.

When using formative assessment prompts built into lessons using programs like Nearpod and Poll Everywhere, the questions or prompts are often spaced out instead of being grouped together like an informal quiz. Comparisons to more traditional formative assessments, such as exit quizzes, may come up, prompting questions about which format is more effective. There is no correct number of questions or prompts to include in a formative assessment; the correct number is the amount that gives the teacher enough information to design and implement actionable next steps to address the formative data points. Include too few questions and you will not have enough information to accurately gauge student understanding. Include too many questions and you now have several prompts that will not realistically be addressed in a timely manner, meaning instructional time was taken with formative assessments that will not be fully utilized. As expertise with formative assessments expands, questions and prompts will be designed to offer the maximum actionable data in the minimal amount of time.

••

There is no correct number of questions or prompts to include in a formative assessment; the correct number is the amount that gives the teacher enough information to design and implement actionable next steps to address the formative data points.

••

Checks for Understanding to Inform Small Group Instruction

You can also create checks for understanding to generate formative data in your lesson. As previously mentioned, they should:

- ♦ Only include enough questions or prompts to give you the information you need to inform actionable next steps. Remember that additional questions that are not acted upon required instructional time to administer.

- Not be graded. These are designed to give you and the students the information you need to continue working toward mastery; if mastery is not yet achieved, the actionable next steps should help students get one step closer. An assigned grade sends the message that there is no next step to mastery for this topic and runs counter to the growth mindset approach we are working so hard to instill.

Be cautious with your wording. Calling a formative assessment or check for understanding a "quiz" or a "test" has implications for students; you can refer to formative assessments in any way as long as students clearly understand their role in their learning. This is especially critical when using a quiz program to create formative assessments. One example, Google Forms, is a great way to generate formative data in a lesson. Any Google Form can be turned into a quiz simply by adding an answer key to the survey questions. You can include a variety of questions on the formative assessment, including multiple choice, answer grid, and open-ended short answer.

TECH TIP

You can invite another teacher to build a Google Form-based quiz with you by choosing "add collaborator" from the menu. This facilitates the development of a common formative assessment that can be used by both teachers.

Gathering Formative Data Through Different Learning Modalities

While many formative assessment programs use multiple choice as the primary format because of the ease with which it can generate data, it is important to remember that students have a wide variety of learning modalities, and offering different methods for them to demonstrate mastery is essential in accurately understanding their needs. Some students may not perform as well on traditional assessments but may thrive using other formats, and instructional technology can help facilitate these opportunities. One option to consider is video or audio presentations in which students can create a short video or audio message in response to a prompt and submit it for feedback. They can explain how they solved a problem or discuss the meaning of a passage in a video, which can then be submitted electronically using Google Forms, Flipgrid, or similar programs. Students can also make a very short presentation slidedeck and record their response as they go through the slides. This approach gives students an opportunity to explain their responses in their own words, something that is logistically challenging to do live in class for every student. It also allows them to express their answer in their own words without having an audience, which can cause anxiety for some students. The teacher can approach shy students privately, commend them on their submission, and ask if it can be played for the class. The initial, private validation of the submission can build confidence and make the student more likely to agree, getting them one step closer to responding to prompts live. This builds confidence, prepares students for leadership roles, and creates opportunities for students to connect with the content and each other.

FORMATIVE DATA FOR SOCIAL JUSTICE

Consider asking students to identify elements about their learning modalities, how they learn best, and what response formats they are most comfortable with. Students from different backgrounds will likely have different responses, and creating space for them to share will give you critical insights needed to serve all students while developing students' metacognition.

The main drawback of gathering formative data through a wide variety of formats is the difficulty in rapidly accessing and analyzing the data. Unlike multiple-choice formative assessments, the teacher will need time to review the prompts and determine actionable next steps based on them. In most cases, this will need to be done between class sessions, resulting in differentiated grouping the next day. It is not a heavy price to pay, but it is a drawback nonetheless. The recommendation is to utilize a combination of on-the-fly assessments and planned formative assessments that support a variety of different learning modalities so you have actionable next steps as well as detailed data to review and plan for with colleagues. As the formats become used more regularly, the turnaround time will naturally lessen. Intentionally practicing transitions and analysis practices around formative assessments with students will reduce turnaround time further. Use Figure 4.3 to brainstorm formative assessment prompts that serve differing learning modalities and how

FIGURE 4.3 Formative Assessments for Different Learning Modalities

Description of formative assessment	How its use can benefit different learning modalities	Instructional technology you will use to facilitate this prompt

instructional technology can facilitate their use. Keep in mind that variety is not needed for variety's sake; each approach should have a specific purpose that furthers learning.

Student-Generated Formative Assessments

Finally, students can use instructional technology to generate formative assessments for their peers as a way to extend their own understanding. Sekendiz (2018) explains,

> [Peer assessments are a] collaborative learning method that actively engages the students in the learning process by enabling them to take an active role in the management of their own learning (Butler & Winnie, 1995). According to Kollar and Fischer (2010), this results from the high-level of cognitive processing during feedback provision that requires the assessing student not only to deeply process their peer's work, but also show planning and monitoring concerning how to formulate constructive feedback that can benefit their peer. (p. 683)

In groups, students can design questions and carefully plan answer choices that highlight misconceptions. By discussing the misconceptions, students can demonstrate their own deep understanding and explain their choices. This activity can provide informal formative data to the teacher as he or she joins the conversations, and then provide more information once students answer each group's prepared questions. It should be made clear that the purpose of this activity is to extend everyone's thinking, not to succeed in having other groups answer incorrectly. Students can use programs like Google Forms or polling software to develop the questions.

Key Takeaways

In this chapter, we explored how instructional technology can facilitate the development and implementation of formative assessments that provide information for actionable next steps. We compared the benefits and drawbacks of on-the-fly formative assessments and planned assessments that cater to students' differing learning modalities, and we reviewed how student-generated formative assessments can reveal insights about their mastery levels. In the next chapter, we will look more closely at building student capacity through formative data, which will continue their journey to becoming independent learners.

5
Building Student Capacity Through Formative Data

Part I: The Need to Reevaluate How We Use Data in the Classroom

Changing Instructional Data Considerations Due to ... *(Introduction)*
♦ Advancements in Technology Changing Formative Data Use
♦ Loss of Consistent Summative Data From Previous Academic Years
♦ Concerns About Data Reliability Due to Increased Remote Assessment
♦ Concerns About "Learning Loss" During Distance Learning

Your Classroom's Vision and Beliefs *(Chapter 1)*
♦ Assessing Your Classroom Vision
♦ Reflecting on Your Beliefs About Student Learning and Your Role
♦ Where Formative Data Fits In

The Impact of Formative Data on Student Success *(Chapter 2)*
♦ Formative Data Fosters Students' Growth Mindset
♦ Formative Data Informs Instruction
♦ Formative Data Facilitates Differentiation and Promotes Equity

DOI: 10.4324/9781003246213-8

Part II: Effective Formative Data Use in the New Classroom

Maximizing the Effectiveness of Formative Data (*Chapter 3*)	Using Instructional Technology to Effectively Address Formative Data (*Chapter 4*)	Building Student Capacity Through Formative Data (*Chapter 5*)	Analyzing Formative Data Collaboratively to Identify and Celebrate Best Practices (*Chapter 6*)
♦ How *Actionable* Is the Data You Are Gathering? ♦ How *Timely* Is the Data You Are Gathering? ♦ How Much Data Do You Need?	♦ On-the-Fly Formative Data for Whole Class Instruction ♦ Formative Assessments for Differentiated Learning	♦ Digital Self-Assessment Rubrics ♦ Self-Selected Small Groups ♦ Self-Monitored Digital Success Trackers	♦ PLCs ♦ Peer Observations—In-Person and Virtual ♦ Teacher-Led Professional Development ♦ Success Celebration Events

Innovative Learning in the New Classroom (*Chapter 7*)
♦ Re-envisioning Learning for All Students
♦ Reflecting on the Focus on Summative and Formative Assessments
♦ Preparing Students to Be Lifelong Independent Learners

Up to this point, we have explored in detail the impact that formative data can have on instruction and planning. We have seen how it can provide critical information to classroom teachers on adjusting their instructional plan to meet students' needs. What we have not yet discussed in depth is the information formative data can provide to students. Classrooms with advanced formative data use create opportunities for students to access the data, draw conclusions about their own areas of strength and growth, and identify next steps to advance their learning. They become independent learners who take charge of their own learning and continue to grow as lifelong learners. Historically, students in more affluent communities have more opportunities to develop as independent learners, which ultimately prepares them for leadership positions. Students in lower income neighborhoods, on the other hand, may have more gaps in their learning, which results in an instructional program designed around well-meaning but more structured learning opportunities that are driven by the teacher. By pushing students from all backgrounds to build their capacity as independent learners, we can make tremendous strides in closing the achievement gap. One of the most important ways for us to build this aspect of student learning is to invite them to become active partners in formative data analysis and actionable next steps. Hattie (2012) offers three critical elements for effective assessment and feedback:

- The criteria for evaluating any learning achievements must be made transparent to students to enable them to have a clear overview of the aims of their work and of what it means to complete it successfully.
- Students should be taught the habits and skills of collaboration in peer assessment, both because these are of intrinsic value and because peer assessment can help to develop the objectivity required for effective self-assessment.
- Students should be encouraged to bear in mind the aims of their work and to assess their own progress to meet these aims as they proceed. They will then be able to guide their own work and so become independent learners (Black et al., 2003, 52–3). (p. 128)

This active participation in identifying strengths and areas of focus does not occur naturally, of course. Students must be trained on how to access and understand the data and must understand why they are taking on this responsibility. Similarly, parents and guardians must learn about the importance of building students' capacity with being able to speak to their own learning. For some, their own learning experience will suggest that formative data analysis is solely the teacher's job. They must also understand the nuances in language that come with an independent learner environment. Instead of saying "I'm not good at this," students must learn to use language showing that they have yet to achieve mastery, such as "I am working on mastering this."

Use Figure 5.1 to brainstorm your approach for introducing this concept to students and to parents and guardians.

FIGURE 5.1 Introducing the Independent Learner Philosophy to Stakeholders

Plan your responses to these prompts for your stakeholders	For Students	For Parent/ Guardians
Describe how you will explain what you mean by "independent learner"		
How will you justify its importance in your classroom?		
What will be your role as a teacher in an independent learner-focused classroom?		
How will you support students who need additional guidance?		

Several digital resources can facilitate this transformation in your classroom. In this chapter, we will explore three of them in depth: digital self-assessment rubrics, self-selected small groups, and self-monitored digital success trackers. By implementing these resources in your classroom and training students on how to use them effectively, you will build their capacity to take ownership of their learning using the formative data you provide and ultimately prepare them to become independent learners ready for leadership.

••

One of the most important ways for us to build this aspect of student learning is to invite them to become active partners in formative data analysis and actionable next steps.

••

Digital Self-Assessment Rubrics

A great way to get students comfortable with understanding their own learning is to train them on using self-assessment rubrics.

For any assessment that utilizes a rubric to evaluate, include a space for students to self-rate themselves and justify why they feel they are at that particular level. While this strategy is not specific to formative assessments, it is one of the quickest and easiest ways to get students to reflect on their own understanding and be able to articulate their areas of strength and growth. Consider the rubrics in Figure 5.2: one includes a self-assessment component, and one does not. How will the two result in different outcomes?

With the addition of the two bolded sections, students can now self-rate their progress and have an opportunity to reflect on their needed area of focus. Prompts can also be introduced to explore differences in teacher and student assessments to better understand expectations and the criteria for success. This simple

FIGURE 5.2 Comparing Rubrics

Rubric A: No self-assessment component

	Level 1	Level 2	Level 3	Level 4	Teacher Assessment
Criteria 1					2
Criteria 2					3
Criteria 3					3

Rubric B: With self-assessment component

	Level 1	Level 2	Level 3	Level 4	Self-Assessment	Explain what is needed to move to the next level of mastery	Teacher Assessment
Criteria 1					4		2
Criteria 2					2		3
Criteria 3					3		3

addition included in assessments can build students' capacity to reflect on their own learning and be better prepared to take the lead on the next steps for their learning.

Once students identify their areas of focus using this rubric, they can target their efforts to developing mastery in their area by choosing one of the learning opportunities you provide that fits their need. Researcher Dweck (2010) explains, "Teachers can also ask their students to choose an area in which they would like to improve and then to establish a personal goal that would be a big reach for them" (p. 18). Giving students options to navigate their learning is a critical element in building their capacity as independent learners and offering a personalized learning experience.

This is where instructional technology can come in to create these opportunities. The varying next steps can be posted on your website for students to access. By using a similar process each time, students will become accustomed to accessing the site and the learning activities to address the rubric results. The learning activities can be different, but a similar process each time will minimize transition time and logistical questions. You can also use a cloud-based program like Google sheets to track students' understanding of their own learning over time by assessing their self-rating accuracy, and you can make connections between rubric-based projects and apps you use to build specific skills. Lessons in programs such as i-Ready, Newsela, No Red Ink, and others can be linked to the self-assessment rubrics, leading students to navigate to the appropriate interventions to build the necessary skills.

Throughout this process, students must have opportunities to articulate their strengths, areas of focus, and how they are addressing them so they become comfortable with their role as independent learners. Part of their learning is skill-building, but part of it is also their development as learners. Give them choices in how they can do this. Students can verbally share it in small groups, record a screencast to explain their progress, write a short summary, and more. By investing heavily in this process, you will be making a dramatic impact in closing the achievement gap by offering all students an opportunity to take ownership of their learning as independent learners.

••

Giving students options to navigate their learning is a critical element in building their capacity as independent learners and offering a personalized learning experience.

••

In addition to self-assessment using rubrics, you can give students an opportunity to provide feedback to each other. Of course, extensive training and time spent developing a positive and collaborative classroom culture are prerequisites to ensuring this activity extends thinking. You can establish clear parameters and require explanations for responses. For example, students can respond to a prompt on a cloud-based slidedeck, using one slide to enter their responses, and have another student provide comments and questions. Students can self-assess taking the feedback into account. This provides one more layer of analysis to build students' capacity to understand mastery.

••

FORMATIVE DATA FOR SOCIAL JUSTICE

Formative data gives the teacher critical data to identify learning needs, but it can also provide this information to students as well if they are taught how to use it. Teaching students how to analyze data from their performance and self-monitor progress builds their capacity as independent learners, which is critical for closing achievement gaps, reinforcing growth mindset, and developing lifelong learners.

••

Self-Selected Small Groups

The self-assessment rubrics can also lead to differentiated small groups for intervention or enrichment. These groupings can also be self-selected, but they do not need to be limited to the connection to the rubrics. Students can self-select into small groups based on formative assessment data if they have access to the data points and have been trained on how to interpret them. Bibbens (2018) explains:

> A systematic approach to formative assessment has allowed us to be both more rigorous, as well as more supportive, in our assessment of student work. Progress tracking offers accountability and encouragement, but perhaps the most important effect of the change in combining data tracking with an explicit approach to formative assessment has been the culture shift: a move away from an emphasis on letter grades to an emphasis on improvement. This has allowed us to articulate to students and parents with greater precision what they need to learn in order to improve, and how we intend for them to learn. It places the onus for doing the cognitive work that will lead to learning distinctly upon the student, but it also puts the teacher in a position where they are there to support, encourage, and eventually share in each student's success. (p. 40)

Building students' capacity to take on this activity can dramatically impact their growth mindset as they self-identify their areas of growth and take clear steps on addressing them. Said et al. (2019) also point out that

> Success is not always attainable on assessments on the first attempt. One consideration is student's inbuilt

fear of handling exposure to failure . . . technology-enhanced assessment helps the student to face up to this fear through self-assessment, which shows areas of weaknesses with feedback beforehand that can be self-corrected. (p. 26)

In addition, they add, "Technology-enhanced assessments promote self-directed learning as results and feedback are usually personalised through self-assessments (Sweeney et al., 2017) and not compared with any other student" (Said et al., 2019, p. 28). As mentioned earlier, building students' capacity to self-assess and take charge of their learning is critical in their development as independent learners, one of the most important characteristics we can impact on students before they graduate. Uribe and Vaughan (2017) explain,

> Reflecting on how feedback is furthering student learning should be an essential part of an educator's instructional practice. Having students also reflect on their own understanding of feedback, how it makes them feel, and what action they can take as a result, can also contribute to the process of feeding forward. (p. 299)

Consider how instructional technology can facilitate this process. One approach is to offer a formative assessment digitally and make the results available to students. If the assessment is accessed from your website or a cloud-based document, the next steps for grouping can be shared on that same page. You can use prompts such as "If your formative data reveals that you will build your strength in [insert topic], you can consider joining [group name] or [group name]. If you want additional support in [insert topic], you can join [group name]." Use generic group names so you won't have to create new ones each time. However, avoid using group names such as Group 1, Group 2, Group A, or Group B as those imply that one group is more advanced than others. Instead, use group names based on a classroom theme so they remain neutral. In an English class, for example, group names can be named after authors whose work has been discussed.

As an example, assume you offer a two-prompt formative assessment using Google Forms and include answer choices with misconceptions in both. You can analyze the responses on the spot by filtering them using Google Sheets and see that 85% of the class answered the first prompt correctly and 20% answered the second prompt correctly. Most students who answered incorrectly went for the answer choice with the misconception. In your rotations, you can offer the 85% a video introduction to an application of the concept you have prepared while you review the concept with the 15% who need clarification. The application can be customized for each student with the help of instructional technology. The students are split into four groups—the three groups that make up the 85% follow the teacher-developed next steps video, while the teacher works with the fourth group to review the concept missed. A check for understanding leads to the students in the group transitioning to the video. This process is initially led by the teacher but as students become more accustomed to self-assessing, they can determine which group they join based on their responses and needs. This transition will take time and consistent reinforcement, but the rewards it yields are invaluable. For the second prompt, the teacher considers whole-group review since most of the students struggled with the concepts in that prompt. For the 20% of students who answered correctly, a research-based follow-up prompt is offered to encourage further exploration. In this scenario, the formative data points inform instruction, and differentiated supports help all students progress toward mastery.

Self-selected grouping connects well with the individual rotation blended learning model, which allows students to rotate from one group to another when they have demonstrated mastery instead of in set groups. Starting with this model can be challenging as students may not yet have the expertise to analyze their own understanding. Before adopting this model, train students on using the station rotation model in which students move to different stations for different learning experiences. Gradually expand their opportunities to self-assess and determine their next steps. As they become more comfortable with the process and their self-analysis improves (this is where self-assessment rubrics can build student capacity), you can steadily introduce the individual rotation model. There may be hesitancy to make this shift as giving some of the control to students can initially result in confusion or lost time in transitions, but consistent training and guidance will lead to success. The effort is well worth it as the outcome gives students an opportunity to grow that few classrooms have offered them. Make the investment and watch your students grow.

TECH TIP

Technology does not need to be present in all small groups. You may consider using instructional technology in some groups if it will help facilitate learning, but keep in mind that a blended learning classroom includes learning without devices as well. Use your devices in groups where it will have the greatest impact based on the needs of each group.

Self-Monitored Digital Success Trackers

You can also use digital success trackers to allow students to self-monitor and better understand their progress toward mastery. Sun et al. (2016) explain,

> Teachers sharing performance data with students and explaining to the students how they were doing against

> other schools served as a motivating force for students and helped their scores go up, as reported in a few studies (Cruz 2010; Hamilton et al. 2009; Palucci 2010; Simpson 2011). It allowed them to buy into the instructional program, fostered ownership of the learning process, helped students set their personal learning goals, allowed students to self-monitor their learning, and made them feel good when their scores went up. (p. 19)

To do this, you'll need an inventory of skills, concepts, and practices students need to master. You will also need to identify the success indicators for each skill that students can use to track their progress. Finally, you will need to provide access to performance data and train students on how to interpret it. Putting digital success trackers in action can help students track their progress, celebrate their successes, and articulate their areas of strength and growth. They can also be used to gamify learning, which can increase engagement and interest. "Recent research has found that applying learning analytics to learning activities can improve students' levels of engagement, which can in turn play an essential role in self-regulated learning environments" (Yoo & Jin, 2020, p. 13). As a byproduct, students can develop mastery with data analysis and can learn how to visualize their progress. You can use spreadsheet programs like Microsoft Excel or Google Sheets to get started, eventually providing students with opportunities for customization and deeper analysis. Yoo and Jin (2020) explain:

> When learning data is related to learning objectives and is able to track learners' progress, meaningful visual feedback can be created to enhance desired learning behaviors according to a process model (Verbert et al., 2013). As a result, learners may gain a better overview of discussion activities (*awareness*), reflect on their own activities

(*self-reflection*), find their deficiencies (*sensemaking*), and change their learning behavior to compensate for these deficiencies (*impact*). (p. 2)

 CONNECTION TO COMPANION BOOK

Just as self-monitoring is a critical skill to develop in the classroom, working with school leaders to build their capacity as learners at the organizational level is also important in establishing a culture that prioritizes growth mindset and constant improvement. The companion book explores how teams can lay the groundwork for this organizational culture and how it can lead to dramatic student gains.

Key Takeaways

In this chapter, we learned how digital self-assessment rubrics, self-selected small groups, and self-monitored digital success trackers using instructional technology can significantly extend students' ability to gain a deeper understanding of mastery levels and build their capacity as independent learners. Instructional technology can facilitate the implementation of these best practices to accelerate students' development as engaged independent learners. In the next chapter, we will explore how collaborating with colleagues through systematized and thoughtful formative data analysis can inform the instructional opportunities you can offer students in your classroom.

6

Analyzing Formative Data Collaboratively to Identify and Celebrate Best Practices

Part I: The Need to Reevaluate How We Use Data in the Classroom

Changing Instructional Data Considerations Due to ... *(Introduction)*
♦ Advancements in Technology Changing Formative Data Use
♦ Loss of Consistent Summative Data From Previous Academic Years
♦ Concerns About Data Reliability Due to Increased Remote Assessment
♦ Concerns About "Learning Loss" During Distance Learning

Your Classroom's Vision and Beliefs *(Chapter 1)*
♦ Assessing Your Classroom Vision
♦ Reflecting on Your Beliefs About Student Learning and Your Role
♦ Where Formative Data Fits In

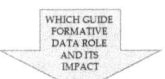

The Impact of Formative Data on Student Success *(Chapter 2)*
♦ Formative Data Fosters Students' Growth Mindset
♦ Formative Data Informs Instruction
♦ Formative Data Facilitates Differentiation and Promotes Equity

DOI: 10.4324/9781003246213-9

Part II: Effective Formative Data Use in the New Classroom

Maximizing the Effectiveness of Formative Data (*Chapter 3*)	Using Instructional Technology to Effectively Address Formative Data (*Chapter 4*)	Building Student Capacity Through Formative Data (*Chapter 5*)	Analyzing Formative Data Collaboratively to Identify and Celebrate Best Practices (*Chapter 6*)
♦ How *Actionable* Is the Data You Are Gathering? ♦ How *Timely* Is the Data You Are Gathering? ♦ How Much Data Do You Need?	♦ On-the-Fly Formative Data for Whole Class Instruction ♦ Formative Assessments for Differentiated Learning	♦ Digital Self-Assessment Rubrics ♦ Self-Selected Small Groups ♦ Self-Monitored Digital Success Trackers	♦ PLCs ♦ Peer Observations—In-Person and Virtual ♦ Teacher-Led Professional Development ♦ Success Celebration Events

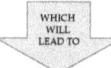

Innovative Learning in the New Classroom (*Chapter 7*)
♦ Re-envisioning Learning for All Students ♦ Reflecting on the Focus on Summative and Formative Assessments ♦ Preparing Students to Be Lifelong Independent Learners

In the previous chapters, we examined the power of formative data points in your classrooms, particularly when they are used with instructional technology to inform instruction and build student capacity for independent learning. The strategies and resources shared have been limited to a single classroom up to this point, but now we are ready to explore the extended possibilities with formative data points when they transcend between classrooms and instructors. Our colleagues have best practices to share, and we must also share ours with them so all students can benefit. Also, note that up to this point, our focus has been on identifying areas of strength and growth, not on potential strategies to address growth areas once students are in small groups; our colleagues may have proven strategies for our particular areas of need. Building a professional network in which we can share ideas, look at data together to make meaning and identify trends, and tackle challenges together is an essential step in developing a culture of collaboration and common vision. In this chapter, we will explore ways to build this community.

PLCs

Professional learning communities, or PLCs, are among the most popular collaborative networks. Popularized by Richard DuFour, PLCs are teams of teachers who meet on a regular basis to discuss instruction, engage in cycles of inquiry, and collaboratively look at student data. PLCs are highly effective when the team develops and implements common formative assessments (CFAs) to review the data together. Reviewing the assessment data can help identify actionable next steps to address student areas of growth. For example, if two teachers administer the same CFA, they can review the results together to see how students performed; if one teacher's students struggled with a particular prompt that the other teacher's students excelled in, the teachers can discuss the approach the teacher took that resulted in the high performance on that prompt. The other teacher can then use that approach during small group review. It is an incredible advantage to be working with another educator and having access to instructional approaches that have been successful and are backed by assessment data.

••

Building a professional network in which we can share ideas, look at data together to make meaning and identify trends, and tackle challenges together is an essential step in developing a culture of collaboration and common vision.

••

This collaborative approach can yield tremendous gains in student mastery for both teachers, yet we do not see this PLC method utilized as regularly as it should. What prevents teachers from establishing PLCs at every school? There are several potential factors, some of which can be alleviated with technology. First, some teachers are hesitant to show their student results to other teachers out of embarrassment over student errors. This feeling can occur because as educators, we equate our success with our students' success, and their failure can be interpreted as our own failure, something we may want to keep to ourselves. This can be addressed with a concerted effort to establish a positive school culture that fosters growth mindset in the faculty and encourages critical data analysis for the benefit of all students. We must believe that we can continuously improve our practice and that we have best practices that others can benefit from. This shift in culture will not come overnight, but consistent messaging coupled with creating space for educators to connect will help schools move toward opening up to the PLC concept. Use Figure 6.1 to reflect on your school's current collaborative culture.

FIGURE 6.1 Your School's Collaborative Culture

	By You	By Your Colleagues
How collaboration with formative data is perceived		
Familiarity with PLCs		
Willingness to share formative data		
Belief that you have best practices others can benefit from		
Potential hurdles needed to overcome to establish PLCs		

Second, teachers often do not have time allotted to collaborate in PLCs. PLCs are only effective if they are a regular part of teachers' practice. PLCs and common formative data must be prioritized, which can only be demonstrated by setting aside time to make it happen. Sporadic PLC meetings will have little impact as collaborative data analysis gets limited time. Find time to meet regularly and schedule the meetings in advance for the year to establish PLCs as a normal part of professional development. Sharing the benefits with your administrative leaders will hopefully persuade them to build PLCs in their professional development plan for the year.

A third challenge is not having a colleague who teaches the same course as you, which limits your ability to develop and administer CFAs. This scenario often occurs in smaller schools or for courses typically taught by one teacher on campus such as AP Physics. Fortunately, the dramatic increase in technology access and comfort can address this challenge by facilitating virtual meetings with teachers on other campuses. A few years ago, the idea of videoconferencing with a colleague in another school may have been a foreign concept, but with our newfound comfort with apps like Zoom, it is easier than ever to collaborate virtually with educators on other campuses. Technology can also facilitate the development of CFAs with teachers on and off your campus. You can use cloud-based programs to collaboratively build CFAs that multiple teachers will administer in order to have common data to discuss during the next PLC. These steps will no doubt take some time to implement, but their benefit on student learning cannot be overemphasized. Find partners who will join you in this venture to maximize the impact of your instructional practice.

CONNECTION TO COMPANION BOOK

Using PLCs with school leaders at the organizational level is also discussed in the companion book. PLCs are a great approach for reviewing data, identifying takeaways, and developing next steps to address them. Teachers have unmatched insight into students' needs and backgrounds and should be integral members of any PLC team, including at the organizational level.

Peer Observations—In-Person and Virtual

Another practice that will inform your instruction is peer observation. As educators, we often do not have the space to visit other classrooms and learn from each other, yet each visit can yield powerful takeaways that we can apply in our classrooms. Peer observations positively impact both the observer and the teacher being observed if a feedback protocol is utilized and provided. The observing teacher sees effective instructional practice in action to help solidify the concepts shared in professional development sessions, while the teacher observed benefits from insights through the feedback protocol. The observer can witness how instructional strategies discussed in PLCs are implemented, leading to deeper understanding and more efficient application. If a picture is worth a thousand words, an observation may be worth a million. Hattie's (2009) research on the factors that impact student achievement confirms this. Based on his findings, he explains, "The four types of instruction found to be most effective on teacher knowledge and behavior were: observation of actual classroom methods; microteaching; video/audio feedback; and practice" (p. 120).

Before the observation, discuss what formative data–related practice you will look for and ask any preliminary questions to get the most of the observation. Peer observations are most effective when they are short and frequent; an extensive observation often provides too much information to apply all at once. To maximize the impact for both the observer and the teacher being observed, schedule a short debrief after each observation. These should typically be within 48 hours of the observation so the findings can be discussed while they are still fresh; a good practice is to schedule the debrief before you complete the observation. If trust has been established and the teacher allows it, consider videotaping the observation so you can reference it later. In the debrief, ask probing questions about the methods used and how they met the needs of all students. These observations are meant to enhance the instructional practice of everyone involved and must be grounded in a growth mindset in order to be effective. They are not evaluative or critical in nature; trust must be established to ensure honesty and vulnerability.

One of the hurdles teachers face is finding coverage in order to conduct the observation. To create opportunities for observations, talk to your administration team about coverage. While substitute teachers can fulfill this task, administrators can also provide coverage. Not only does this latter option simplify the logistics with arranging an observation, it gives administrators a rare opportunity to step back into the classroom. This can help them stay connected to their instructional experience and build empathy with the faculty team.

••

If a picture is worth a thousand words, an observation may be worth a million.

••

••

                    TECH TIP

Virtual peer observations can be implemented live through videoconferencing programs such as Zoom or Google Meet if cameras are set up in locations to facilitate observations, but they can also be viewed asynchronously if the lesson is recorded. In either case, be sure proper permission has been granted by anyone who will be in the virtual observation.

••

Teacher-Led Professional Development

Teacher-led professional development is yet another way that teachers can learn about effective formative data analysis and its impact on instructional practice. Administrators are instructional leaders, but that role does not need to remain exclusively theirs. Giving teachers an opportunity to share their best practices can help teachers build leadership capacity while giving others valuable tools to apply in their own classrooms. Indeed,

> a PD program is only as effective as how well it is received by participants. One of the best ways to increase buy-in, engagement, and credibility is to co-plan and co-lead PD with teachers and other classroom practitioners. Doing so builds their leadership capacity, while reinforcing the notion that training is closely tied and applicable to classrooms. (Mekhitarian, 2021, p. 29)

Collaborating with administrators to co-develop and co-lead the trainings can also make stronger connections between the faculty and administration and reinforce the notion that everyone on campus is working toward the common goal of student success. Different teachers should be given the opportunity to share best practices to avoid the appearance of preference and to foster a culture of shared leadership. All professional development

> must be driven by effective instructional practices but be able to incorporate technology tools and programs when applicable. Sessions that focus solely on technological resource sharing have not proven to be the most effective form of PD; teachers need context to know how the technology can apply to instruction and student learning. Student learning—the ultimate outcome of teacher growth—must drive PD, with technology supporting that focus. The two should always be presented together. (Mekhitarian, 2021, p. 45)

Use Figure 6.2 to reflect on how you can engage your administrative team with supporting peer observations and teacher-led professional development.

FIGURE 6.2 Getting the Administrative Team to Buy In

	Peer Observations	Teacher-Led PD
Current usage at your school		
Trust level to implement		
Potential benefit as perceived by faculty and admin		
What steps are needed to implement		
Proposed timing before first implementation		

IMPLEMENTATION TIP

As mentioned earlier, teachers have critical insights into students' experiences and should be considered essential members of the professional development team. However, their commitment to the classroom can create a logistical hurdle when scheduling time to meet to develop training opportunities. Schedule training planning meetings in advance and plan logistics to allow teachers to join the planning team.

Success Celebration Events

Finally, consider adding success celebration events to highlight student gains with formative data as evidence. These events can build positive school culture; magnify the importance of formative data in instructional practice; develop trust between teachers, students, and administration; and facilitate the sharing of best practices. Make them a regular part of each school year so they become part of the school culture, reinforcing the importance of growth mindset as students show progress toward mastery. It can also build confidence, encourage interaction, and help students feel more connected to the school, all elements of positive socioemotional growth. Parents and guardians can attend both in person and virtually to magnify the impact of the events.

There is no one way to create these events, but regardless of the approach taken, steps taken to achieve the gains must be highlighted so participants can benefit from the best practices. One option is to show the specific area of growth you focused on and how you used formative data to inform your instructional plan to improve student mastery. Video of your implementation in the classroom can accompany your presentation to bring the strategies to life. Students can also present on their gains by sharing their self-monitored student success trackers described in the previous chapter. Allowing students to take the lead builds their capacity as independent learners and their confidence as learners who can continuously grow. Utilize technology to make the event engaging and dazzling. Presentations can include video, live chats, graphical displays of gains, and student-developed projects. The first event will take effort to plan and execute, but as the celebrations become a regular part of school culture, they will become easier to set up. Hesitation about events taking up instructional time will dissipate as students' gains are highlighted and they become skilled independent learners in charge of their education.

CONNECTION TO COMPANION BOOK

In the companion book, we explore how these celebration events can be set up at the organizational level to highlight the successes of students and to share best practices—with formative data backup—that can be replicated by other schools for the benefit of all students in the organization. Multiple data points will be addressed in addition to academic performance, such as attendance and socioemotional data.

Key Takeaways

In this chapter, we explored the benefits of analyzing formative data collaboratively to identify and celebrate best practices through professional learning communities, in-person and virtual peer observations, teacher-led professional development, and success celebration events. Formative data and instructional technology can be used in countless ways to enhance student learning, and we do not need to develop them all on our own: we can accelerate our development as highly effective educational practitioners by collaborating and learning from each other. Technology can facilitate this sharing of ideas to bring effective formative data analysis and utilization to every classroom if we are open to collaboration. Unlike working in isolation in our classrooms, these strategies require a great deal of trust and an unwavering belief that all teachers are working toward the common goal of enhancing student learning. Only when educators commit to working together toward this common goal will they open their practice for others to see and learn from.

7
Innovative Learning in the New Classroom

Part I: The Need to Reevaluate How We Use Data in the Classroom

Changing Instructional Data Considerations Due to . . . (Introduction)
♦ Advancements in Technology Changing Formative Data Use
♦ Loss of Consistent Summative Data From Previous Academic Years
♦ Concerns About Data Reliability Due to Increased Remote Assessment
♦ Concerns About "Learning Loss" During Distance Learning

Your Classroom's Vision and Beliefs (Chapter 1)
♦ Assessing Your Classroom Vision
♦ Reflecting on Your Beliefs About Student Learning and Your Role
♦ Where Formative Data Fits In

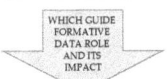

The Impact of Formative Data on Student Success (Chapter 2)
♦ Formative Data Fosters Students' Growth Mindset
♦ Formative Data Informs Instruction
♦ Formative Data Facilitates Differentiation and Promotes Equity

DOI: 10.4324/9781003246213-10

114 ◆ Effective Formative Data Use

Part II: Effective Formative Data Use in the New Classroom

Maximizing the Effectiveness of Formative Data (Chapter 3)	Using Instructional Technology to Effectively Address Formative Data (Chapter 4)	Building Student Capacity Through Formative Data (Chapter 5)	Analyzing Formative Data Collaboratively to Identify and Celebrate Best Practices (Chapter 6)
◆ How *Actionable* Is the Data You Are Gathering? ◆ How *Timely* Is the Data You Are Gathering? ◆ How Much Data Do You Need?	◆ On-the-Fly Formative Data for Whole Class Instruction ◆ Formative Assessments for Differentiated Learning	◆ Digital Self-Assessment Rubrics ◆ Self-Selected Small Groups ◆ Self-Monitored Digital Success Trackers	◆ PLCs ◆ Peer Observations—In-Person and Virtual ◆ Teacher-Led Professional Development ◆ Success Celebration Events

Innovative Learning in the New Classroom (Chapter 7)
◆ Re-envisioning Learning for All Students ◆ Reflecting on the Focus on Summative and Formative Assessments ◆ Preparing Students to Be Lifelong Independent Learners

Up to this point, we have taken a close look at how formative data points used in conjunction with technology can enhance learning and build student capacity as independent learners and how collaborating with other educators can accelerate our instructional practice to increase supports for students. These actions cannot occur effectively on a campus without positive school culture and an established sense of trust. Moreover, a clear schoolwide vision centered on equity, growth mindset, and independent learning is critical in implementing these strategies in every classroom, particularly through collaborative efforts such as professional learning communities and peer observations. Review the classroom vision you developed in Figure 1.2 in the first chapter, and reflect on how it compares to the schoolwide vision—is there coherence between the two to facilitate connections between practitioners? Use Figure 7.1 to guide your thinking.

FIGURE 7.1 Your Classroom Vision Compared to the School's Vision

Your classroom vision from Figure 1.2	Your school's vision	How the two compare/contrast	Your school's readiness for a common focus on formative data

If there is strong alignment, you are ready to make connections and begin reaching out to other teachers and the leadership team to propose collaborative analysis of formative data and instructional best practices. If there is a material disconnect, you will need to identify commonalities and build on them to create the ties necessary for collaborative work. This will take time and will not be easy. How can we convince other experts in the field to examine their approach—perhaps an approach that has been developed over many years—in order to expand formative data use to impact student mastery?

Interestingly, a great way to show the benefits of formative data use is to show data demonstrating its effectiveness. It is easier to make the case for a particular strategy when there is ample evidence that it works. Begin by implementing the formative data analysis and action strategies described in this book, and carefully document their successes. Since you will be using instructional technology, develop a system to regularly store and summarize student gains. Also, develop a system to organize and manage the student self-monitored digital success trackers described in Chapter 5 as those will provide ample evidence of their increasing mastery levels.

Raw data will not be enough to persuade everyone to consider the benefits of collaborative formative data use: an emotional connection must also be made. As educators, we are passionate about student learning and are driven by our desire to see our students grow and succeed; students are our focus, not numbers on a page. Ask students to share from their experience with formative data to connect the data points to authentic student experiences. Give other educators a chance to see the joy of students who have benefited from your practice with formative data analysis. Explain how the celebration events can give students—particularly students who have historically struggled in school—a chance to share their excitement for learning and elation over demonstrating mastery. Engage them in conversations about the potential of a schoolwide commitment to formative data analysis and implementation using instructional technology, and you will get more and more teachers on board with the idea. Bring your ideas together under the theme of equity and access, the critical goals all teachers are committed to.

Re-envisioning Learning for All Students

As you re-envision your classroom with a stronger emphasis on formative data use through instructional technology, consider how your plan will impact each and every student. The main purpose of formative assessments is to provide the necessary data to differentiate supports and provide each student with the learning experiences required to ensure their success. Instructional technology helps personalize this experience at the individual student level by offering levels of customization beyond one level of intervention and one level of enrichment. Together, formative data and instructional technology can serve as catalysts for new levels of equity and access, goals all educators strive for but that require extensive vigilance to apply consistently.

....

As educators, we are passionate about student learning and are driven by our desire to see our students grow and succeed; students are our focus, not numbers on a page.

....

Imagine how your classroom vision will facilitate equity and access. The two require very specific planning to implement, both involving differentiation. Let's start with equity: we know that equity is not the same as equality. Equality means every student gets the same supports, whereas equity means every student gets the supports they need to be successful. These supports will vary based on student needs, which is at the core of differentiation. How will you share this concept with your students, and how will you use this concept to build a classroom culture that focuses on every student's success? In a formative data–based classroom with differentiated learning opportunities and supports, students will quickly notice that their experience can vary from other students in the classroom. For many, this will be a dramatic departure from what they have been used to experiencing through their educational journey, and addressing this change directly can address the confusion as well as build a strong classroom culture around every student succeeding. Share that your goal as a classroom teacher is not to use the same strategies for every student but rather to use any strategy necessary to ensure that each and every student succeeds, even if those strategies differ from one student to the next; that is how you prioritize equity in your classroom.

To ensure equity in the classroom, you must also ensure access. Students cannot be successful if they cannot access the content or the supports. Ensuring access requires multiple levels of support, each critical for an equity-focused classroom that prioritizes each individual student's path to success. These supports include access to technology and other resources and access to training on how to use them. Consider the resources students need to access regularly for success, both at home and in the classroom. In additional to traditional instructional resources such as textbooks, students need consistent access to instructional technology, which requires both a computing device and regular internet access at home. If students do not have access to them at home, they will not have equitable access to instructional resources such as collaborative documents, formative data, and recorded lessons. They also won't have access to technology that can help with translations, research, and visualizations, which can all support understanding.

Access also includes providing the necessary training to maximize the impact of the resources. Be sure to develop systems that provide a variety of supports for using the resources. This includes direct training, peer support teams, and student-accessed guides for technology usage. An effective approach is to create screencasts showing how to use a variety of resources and putting them all on one site for easy access. Students can access this site by scanning a QR code posted in the classroom or typing in a simplified website; you can generate QR codes using countless QR code generator sites free of charge and create shortened web addresses using sites like Tiny URL or Bitly. Establishing peer teams who can provide support with technical issues can also help increase access and minimize lost instructional time. Students will quickly build expertise and require less technical support, especially as they regularly access the resources you have made available to them. From their research, Mitten et al. (2017) concluded,

> Because the apps were a regular part of their instruction, students were familiar with how to use each app and classroom norms had been established early in the year so that collecting data from students was a quick, streamlined process. Student performance results and teacher feedback could be provided to students and parents faster than handwriting feedback and returning to students, in some cases. The use of technology was also viewed as being an effective approach to engage students and parents in the formative assessment process. (p. 12)

Some of these supports can be co-developed with other teachers to lessen the load, such as creating support screencasts for various technical resources; consider reaching out to partners who may be interested in collaborating.

••

Share that your goal as a classroom teacher is not to use the same strategies for every student but rather to use any strategy necessary to ensure that each and every student succeeds, even if those strategies differ from one student to the next; that is how you prioritize equity in your classroom.

••

Once you have established a clear vision for equity and access and the necessary supports to bring them to life in your classroom, you now have a learning environment ready for formative data analysis and action. Students are prepared for differentiation and understand that all activities, resources, and supports in your classroom are designed for one thing: to ensure all students succeed. They understand that these activities, resources, and supports may be differentiated, and they understand why they may differ. With this knowledge of differentiation, students understand the *why* behind formative data, making them far more ready and eager to embrace your philosophy on growth mindset and building students' capacity as independent learners. Your classroom has been re-imagined with a clear focus on formative data.

••

FORMATIVE DATA FOR SOCIAL JUSTICE

Effective formative data use facilitates innovative learning opportunities built on differentiated supports that can maximize learning to close achievement gaps. Do not shy away from employing innovation to create learning opportunities to meet students' needs. Instructional technology is a relatively new resource in the history of public education, and many of its benefits have yet to be cultivated; it is imperative that we employ innovation to ensure all students succeed.

••

Reflecting on the Focus on Summative and Formative Assessments

The COVID-19 pandemic resulted in a sudden pause on summative assessments and data, leading many educators who were used to analyzing their results to shift to a greater focus on formative data. Formative data points are typically more actionable because of their timeliness and frequency, but what role should summative data points play in instruction as they return after the pandemic? Summative data points can continue to inform planning before the school year begins, but their infrequent nature makes them naturally less actionable on a daily basis. Instead, summative assessments should become more formal opportunities to celebrate successes. As a teacher, I utilized summative assessments when the formative assessments administered throughout the unit gave me enough information to be convinced that my students were ready for a summative assessment; administering a summative assessment when the data points showed that additional time and supports were necessary for students to develop mastery felt counterproductive. With heightened use of instructional technology, the timely benefits and subsequent supports offered by formative assessments are magnified further, making summative assessment seem even less connected to informing instruction. Consider connecting summative assessments to the success celebration events described in Chapter 6. Once your students are ready for a summative assessment, make that a culminating activity, and define it as an opportunity for students to show their mastery, which will later be showcased at the celebration event.

....

 CONNECTION TO COMPANION BOOK

In both books, there is a clear focus on formative assessments and data over summative because formative data is consistently actionable and timely. While summative data is considered "high stakes" and often commands more attention, targeting formative data is the way to improve summative results. Focus your efforts on seeing gains in formative data at both the classroom and the organizational level, and the summative data will inevitably be addressed as well.

Preparing Students to Be Lifelong Independent Learners

Combining a clear focus on equity and access with an unwavering focus on formative data over summative data sets up your classroom for independent learning. As discussed in Chapter 5, a focus on independent learning is one of the critical differences between many schools in affluent neighborhoods and schools in lower socioeconomic communities. As part of our commitment to social justice, we must prioritize building students' capacity as independent learners, not as an ideal benefit but as a critical driver of our planning and focus. Regarding students as independent learners involves re-envisioning our roles as educators. Giving students more autonomy and choice over their learning while training them to analyze, understand, and act on their progress data requires a shift in educator roles from teacher to facilitator of learning. As facilitators of learning, we create the learning experiences for students to access and provide supports as needed to guide them through their learning. The heavy lifting occurs prior to the lesson as we use our pedagogical expertise to create learning opportunities that push thinking, offer differentiation, and engage students; the students do the heavy lifting in the classroom as they take ownership of their learning. This is a stark change from the teacher-led classrooms we are accustomed to seeing and ones that most of us experienced as students. This shift requires a strong commitment to developing students' growth mindset and ensuring that students take charge of their learning with our guidance and encouragement. This is not an easy change to make but one that can literally make a lifetime of difference for our students as they become well-equipped to take on leadership positions and continue beyond school as lifelong learners who believe in their continuous ability to grow. In your re-envisioned classroom, you are taking on the role of an active observer in addition to an active learner to allow students to take ownership of their learning.

··

As part of our commitment to social justice, we must prioritize building students' capacity as independent learners, not as an ideal benefit but as a critical driver of our planning and focus.

··

Key Takeaways

In this chapter, we explored how the philosophies and strategies described in the first six chapters can lead to a re-envisioned classroom that shifts the role of the teacher to develop students as independent learners and ensures equity and access for all students. This approach to learning is one that every student will want to be in because it prioritizes the needs of each of them, no matter how different they may be. It is an environment that offers engagement and positive support and one that considers failures as gateways to more opportunities to demonstrate mastery. Work in this classroom is not completed until every student achieves mastery, and this model of continuous growth transforms students' experiences as well as teachers'. It is precisely the type of classroom we would highlight to others and recommend to parents. Let us work together to make this re-envisioned classroom a reality, not just for our own classroom, but for all classrooms serving students.

Conclusion

We have taken an extensive look at the potential impact of formative data on student achievement, particularly through instructional technology and a vision for equity and access. This journey took us through the changing instructional data landscape due to advancements in technology changing formative data use, the loss of consistent summative data from previous academic years due to the COVID-19 pandemic, and concerns about data reliability due to increased remote assessments and "learning loss" during distance learning. Addressing the needs generated by these events required re-envisioning your classroom's vision, including reflecting on your beliefs about student learning, your role in the classroom, and where formative data fits in.

We saw how formative data points can foster students' growth mindset, inform instruction, facilitate differentiation, and promote equity. However, their effectiveness is maximized only when their use is timely, their results are actionable, and just enough is collected at one time to be utilized to minimize lost instructional time. We also explored the dramatic impact formative data points can have on students' development as independent learners if they are given opportunities to take ownership of their learning. Examples of strategies to facilitate this include digital self-assessment rubrics, self-selected small groups, and self-monitored digital success trackers.

In addition to developing this expertise in our classrooms, we explored the extended benefits and accelerated growth potential of collaborating with other educators—both on our campus and virtually with teachers at other schools—through a variety of strategies, including professional learning communities, in-person and virtual peer observations, teacher-led professional development, and success celebration events. These opportunities bring together the collective experiences of practitioners so they can all benefit from effective strategies and collaborative analysis of common formative assessments.

Together, these concepts set the framework for a re-envisioned classroom that for many teachers differs from the classrooms they experienced as students. It is one that fosters growth mindset, encourages innovation through instructional technology use, views each misconception as a concept not yet mastered, and prepares students to be lifelong independent learners.

The potential impact of these concepts on students long after they leave our classrooms is immensely exciting. We have the power to incorporate many of these strategies and philosophies in our own classrooms with issue, but creating systems that impact all students on campus requires buy-in from other educators, a common vision for data-informed instructional practice, and a plan for collaborative leadership. A deeper exploration on how to develop a culture of collaborative formative data use can be found in this book's companion, *Harnessing Formative Data for K-12 Leaders*. That book addresses many of the concepts addressed in this book but focuses on them at the organizational level to bring about schoolwide or districtwide change and benefit all students. Systems for efficiently gathering and acting on schoolwide data points are discussed, as are organizational structures for collaboration over formative data and cycles of inquiry. Combining the practices discussed in this book at the classroom level with the organizational level strategies in the companion book will transform the educational experience of students and prepare them as lifelong independent learners.

References

Anderson, S., Leithwood, K., & Strauss, T. (2010). Leading data use in schools: Organizational conditions and practices at the school and district levels. *Leadership and Policy in Schools*, *9*(3), 292–327.

Beck, J., Morgan, J., Brown, N., Whitesides H., & Riddle, D. (2020). "Asking, learning, seeking out": An exploration of data literacy for teaching. *The Educational Forum*, *84*(2), 150–165.

Bibbens, T. (2018). Learning-driven data: Tracking improvement within a formative assessment cycle in English. *English in Australia*, *53*(1), 33–41.

Cakir, R., Korkmaz, O. Bacanak, A., & Arslan, O. (2016). An exploration of the relationship between students' preferences for formative feedback and self-regulated learning skills. *Malaysian Online Journal of Educational Sciences*, *4*(4), 14–30.

Chanpet, P., Chomsuwan, K., & Murphy, E. (2018). Online project-based learning and formative assessment. *Technology, Knowledge and Learning*, *25*, 685–705.

Chung, G., Shel, T., & Kaiser, W. (2006). An exploratory study of a novel online formative assessment and instructional tool to promote students' circuit problem solving. *The Journal of Technology, Learning, and Assessment*, *5*(6), 1–27.

Cusi, A., Morselli, F., & Sabena, C. (2017). Promoting formative assessment in a connected classroom environment: Design and implementation of digital resources. *Mathematics Education*, *49*, 755–767.

Dalby, D., & Swan, M. (2019). Using digital technology to enhance formative assessment in mathematics classrooms. *British Journal of Educational Technology*, *50*(2), 832–845.

Dudek, C., Reddy, L., Lekwa, A., Hua, A., & Fabiano, G. (2019). Improving universal classroom practices through teacher formative assessment and coaching. *Assessment for Effective Intervention*, *44*(2), 81–94.

Dweck, C. (2007). Boosting achievement with messages that motivate. *Education Canada*, *47*(2), 6–10.

Dweck, C. (2010). Even geniuses work hard. *Educational Leadership*, *68*(1), 16–20.

Finnegan, L., Miller, K., Randolph, K., & Bielskus-Barone, K. (2019). Supporting student knowledge using formative assessment and universal design for learning expression. *The Journal of Special Education Apprenticeship*, *8*(2), 1–14.

Hattie, J. (2009). *Visible learning: A synthesis of over 800 meta-analysis relating to achievement*. Routledge.

Hattie, J. (2012). *Visible learning for teachers: Maximizing impact on learning*. Routledge.

Jeong, J., Gonzalez-Gomez, D., & Yllana Prieto, F. (2020). Sustainable and flipped STEM education: Formative assessment online interface for observing pre-service teachers' performance and motivation. *Educational Sciences*, *10*(283), 1–14.

Jorno, R., & Gynther, K. (2018). What constitutes an "actionable insight" in learning analytics? *Journal of Learning Analytics*, *5*(3), 198–221.

Luckin, R., Clark, W., Avramides, K., Hunter, J., & Martin, O. (2017). Using teacher inquiry to support technology-enhanced formative assessment: A review of the literature to inform a new method. *Interactive Learning Environments*, *25*(1), 85–97.

Mekhitarian, S. (2021). *The essential blended learning PD planner: Where classroom practice meets distance learning*. Corwin Press.

Mitten, C., Jacobbe, T., & Jacobbe, E. (2017). What do they understand? Using technology to facilitate formative assessment. *Australian Primary Mathematics Classroom*, *22*(1), 9–12.

Nicholson, J., Capitelli, S., Richert, A., Wilson, C., & Bove, C. (2017). Teacher leaders building foundations for data-informed teacher learning in one urban elementary school. *The New Educator*, *13*(2), 170–189.

Nyland, R. (2018). A review of tools and techniques for data-enabled formative assessment. *Journal of Educational Technology Systems*, *46*(4), 505–526.

Onodipe, G., & Ayadi, M. (2020). Using smartphones for formative assessment in the flipped classroom. *Journal of Instructional Pedagogies*, *23*, 1–20.

Robertson, S., Humphrey, S., & Steele, J. (2019). Using technology tools for formative assessments. *Journal of Educators Online, 16*(2), 1–10.

RR, S., Fox-Turnbull, W., Earl-Rinehart, K., & Calder, N. (2020). Development of formative assessment tool for a primary, technology classroom. *Design and Technology Journal: An International Journal, 25*(2), 101–116.

Sahin, M. (2019). Classroom response systems as a formative assessment tool: Investigation into students' perceived usefulness and behavioural intention. *International Journal of Assessment Tools in Education, 6*(4), 693–705.

Said, M., Aravind, V., Ferdinand-James, D., & Umachandran, K. (2019). Dissecting assessment: A paradigm shift towards technology-enhanced assessments. *World Journal on Educational Technology: Current Issues, 11*(2), 24–32.

Schmid, D. (2012). Data mining: A systems approach to formative assessment. *Journal of Dance Education, 12*(3), 75–81.

Schmitz, K. (2019). Quality or quantity: Completion rewards and formative assessments in flipped instruction classes. *International Journal for the Scholarship of Teaching and Learning, 13*(3), 1–8.

Sekendiz, B. (2018). Utilisation of formative peer-assessment in distance online education: A case study of a multi-model sport management unit. *Interactive Learning Environments, 26*(5), 682–694.

Shirley, M., & Irving, K. (2014). Connected classroom technology facilitates multiple components of formative assessment practice. *Journal of Science Education and Technology, 24*, 56–58.

Sun, J., Przybylski, R., & Johnson, B. (2016). A review of research on teachers' use of student data: From the perspective of school leadership. *Educational Assessment, Evaluation and Accountability, 28*, 5–33.

Troy, T., & Bulgakov-Cooke, D. (2013). Formative assessment with technology 2011–12: Second year of implementation. *Eye on Evaluation: Data and Accountability Department, 13*(5), 1–30.

Uribe, S., & Vaughan, M. (2017). Facilitating student learning in distance education: A case study on the development and implementation of a multifaceted feedback system. *Distance Education, 38*(3), 288–301.

Vasquez, A., Nussbaum, M., Sciarresi, E., Martınez, T., Barahona, C., & Strasser, K. (2017). The impact of the technology used in formative assessment: The case of spelling. *Journal of Educational Computing Research*, *54*(8), 1142–1167.

Yoo, M., & Jin, S. (2020). Development and evaluation of learning analytics dashboards to support online discussion activities. *Educational Technology & Society*, *23*(2), 1–18.

Index

Note: Page numbers in *italics* indicate figures and page numbers in **bold** indicate tables.

academic performance, data points 110
achievement gap, closure 13, 93
actionable data: access, ease 6, 55–57; access, technology (usage) 8; actionability, determination 54–63; identification 11–12; instructional technology, usage 62–63; points, prompts results 13; providing, instructional technology (usage) 71; student understanding 57–62; timing, determination 65–66
actionable feedback, basis 37
actionable formative data, importance 54–55
actionable next steps: focus 53; potency, loss 64
administrators, collaboration 108
after-school sessions, power 37
analysis paralysis 52–53
answer grid, usage 81
artifacts, project/co-construction goal 27
assessment: access 95; continuous assessment, effectiveness 64; data, validity 15; elements 89
assigned grade, message 81
at-risk students (success), assessment time (impact) 67
attendance: data points 110; organizational level analysis factor 42

best practices (identification/celebration), formative data (collaborative analysis) 102

blended learning: classroom, elements 97; model, consideration 24
block schedule, usage 67
Bloom's Taxonomy, usage 44
brainstorming 83, 90

change, difficulty 5
classroom: beliefs 19; discussions, engineering 29; equity, ensuring 117; formative data use, effectiveness **20**; instruction/assessment, formative data points 42; methods, observation 106; on-the-fly formative assessments, usage 73; pedagogy, formative assessments (impact) 70; progress, evidence 38; self-monitoring skill, development 99; topic mastery, requirement 58
classroom culture: design 63; vision, impact 20
classroom equity: formative data, impact 45; prioritization 119
classroom vision: application 25; assessment 20–26; development *25*; elements, collection *32*; equitable classroom vision *26*; focus 30; impact 116–117; language, inclusion 25; school vision, comparison *115*; usage 26
class-wide data, display 59
clickers, usage 79
cloud-based document, usage 95
cloud-based programs, usage 105
cognitive processing 84

collaboration: culture, development 102–103; habits/skills, student instruction 89; increase 24
collaborative culture *104*
collaborative data review (facilitation), Google Sheets (usage) 66
collaborative learning method 84
common formative assessments (CFAs), team development/ implementation 103
common vision, culture 102–103
concept/skill, student understanding (determination) 60
constructive feedback: formulation 84; perception, problems 64–65; receiving 30
constructivism, usage 21
content (student access), technology (usage) 46
continuous assessment, effectiveness 64
COVID-19 pandemic, impact 3, 120

data: access, student opportunities (creation) 88; actionability, timing (determination) 65–66; collective activity 53; examination 103; interpretation, usage 41; perspective 5; principals, enabler role 53; reliability (concerns), remote assessment increase (impact) 5, 15; review, PLC approach 105; student exposure, usefulness 58
data analysis: critical data analysis, encouragement 104; philosophy, resetting/rethinking 3; plans, usage 3; student instruction 93
data collection: opportunities, instructional technology (usage) 8–11; requirement 46; time, amount 68; timeliness, determination 64–65
data-driven instructional planning, timeliness/actionability 14
data-driven scaffolding/supports, incorporation 28

data-informed decision making, usage 16
data points: actionable data, identification 11–12; collection/ analysis 56; collection, problems 67; continuity disruption, events/ standards change (impact) 14–15; impact 6
data usage: amount, determination 67–68; opportunities, instructional technology (usage) 8–11
diagnostic feedback, providing 64
dialogues, purpose 70–71
differentiated groups/activities, student self-selection 72
differentiated learning: formative assessments, usage 75; opportunities 117
differentiated supports, providing 29
differentiation 71; conversations 10; facilitation, formative data (usage) 42–47; impact 44–45; increase 24; individualized differentiation 74; knowledge 119; maximization, instructional technology (usage) 62–63
digital self-assessment rubrics 90–93; comparison *91*
digital success trackers 90
digital technology, usage 62
discussion activities 98–99
distance learning 14; experience, impact 3, 5; space 15; transition, COVID-19 pandemic (impact) 3

education, assessment-focused approach 39–40
empathy, student usage 60
equitable classroom vision *26*
equity: ensuring 117; equality, contrast 10; facilitation 46; focus 47; formative data, impact 45; formative data, incorporation 47; fostering 54–55; instructional technology, incorporation 47; prioritization 119; promotion, formative data (usage) 42–47

equity-based vision, impact 26–27
equity-focused vision, adoption 51

feedback: actionable feedback, basis 37; collection 72, 73; delay, problems 64–65; diagnostic feedback, providing 64; elements 89; handwriting 118; impact 95; inclusion 37; offering 10; protocol, usage 106; providing 28–29, 54, 64, 72; provision, cognitive processing 84; review 37; video/audio feedback, usage 106; visual feedback, creation 98–99
formative assessment: access, teacher allowance 76; administration 40, 66; advantages 66; brainstorming 83; brevity 58; creation 76; development 65–66; enhancement, technology usage (consideration) 31; focus, reflection 120–121; formats, impact 10; gap, limitation 64; generation, instructional technology (usage) 75–79; higher-order questions, encouragement 15; incorporation 79–80; instructional technology, usage 71; "lean" approach, support 53; learning gains, connection 71; online-based formative assessment interfaces, usage 40; on-the-fly formative assessments, administration 73; platform, selection 76; practices, strategies 29, 30; process, student/parent engagement 118; prompts, inclusion 13; questions/prompts, number (inclusion) 80; reflection 56; responses (analysis), instructional technology (role) 65–66; results 77; scaffolding, usage 27; selection, care 67; sequence, example 78; smartphones, usage 31; student access process 62; student-generated formative assessments 83–84; systematic approach 94; systematic approach, shift 43; understanding 7; usefulness 60; utility, maximization (adoption) 61; value/practice 28
formative assessment usage 61, 71, 75; increase, advocacy 15; limitations 30
formative data: actionable formative data, importance 54–55; addressing, instructional technology (usage) 71; benefits 115; collaborative analysis 103; collection/application (enhancement), technology (usage) 45; current year formative data, instructional plans (basis) 13; effectiveness, maximization 51; gains, efforts (focus) 121; impact 29–32, 39–42; importance 109; incorporation 47; online-based formative data (collection), polling programs (usage) 73; on-the-fly formative data, usage 71–74; organizational formative data analysis, requirements 72–73; prioritization 42; providing 71; real-time access 6; review/discussion 65; sharing (acceleration), technology (usage) 64; steps 4; system, reflection 57; teacher review 77, 79; technology advancements, impact 6–13; technology, usage 11; use, innovative learning opportunities (facilitation) 119
formative data collection: drawback 83; learning modalities, usage 81–83; limitations 55
formative data, focus 120–121; plan, creation 32
formative data points: actionability determination process 55; addressing 80; checks 63
formative data, understanding 7; struggle 44
formative data usage 10, 42–47, 88; effectiveness 43; emphasis 116; understanding 41

formative feedback: providing 72; usefulness 57–58
formative quiz, development 71–72

graduation rate, organizational level analysis factor 42
growth: highlighting 43; mapping 61
growth mindset: approach 81; building 75; culture, formative data points (usage) 38; development 36–37, 121–122; experience *39*; focus 21; fostering, formative data (usage) 36–39; impact 94–95; prioritization 99; reinforcement 93; teacher usage 38; usage 32

higher-order questions, encouragement 15

ideas, sharing 103
improvement, emphasis 94
independent learner: capacity, student building 93; development 30; growth 26–27; philosophy, introduction *90*; student preparation 121–122; vision, usage 32
individualized differentiation, usage 47
innovative learning opportunities, facilitation 119
in-person peer observations 105–107
instruction: assessments, connection 53; educator design 60
instructional data, considerations (change) 3
instructional decision making, data types (usage) 46
instructional plan, constructivism (usage) 21
instructional practice, formative data (importance) 109
instructional program, acceptance 98
instructional resources, usage 29
instructional software, usage 28

instructional technology: consideration 6; impact 92; incorporation 47; introduction 11–12; post-pandemic instructional technology, usage 22; resource 119; role 65–66, 75
instructional technology-led approach, usage 23
instructional technology, usage 8–11, 62–63, 71, 75–79; consideration 97, 115; process 54
instructional time, maximization 13
instructors/learners, interactions 40

keyword programs, usage 74
knowledge: self-assessment 60; teaching/instructing/ transmitting 27

language, usage 59–60
leadership capacity, building 108
learners, progress (tracking) 98–99
learning: advancement, technology (relationship) 24; analytics, impact 6; assessment for learning 7, 41–43; assessment of learning 7, 41–43; assessment (support), technology (impact) 6; backgrounds 25; devices, absence 97; driving 37–38; facilitation, instructional technology-led approach (usage) 23; gains, formative assessment (connection) 71; gamification 98; goal, instruction design (impact) 60; innovations 114; innovative learning opportunities, facilitation 119; intentions, clarifying/ sharing 29; objectives, learning data (relationship) 98–99; opportunities 43; self-regulated learning environments 98; student ownership 29
learning evidence: collection methodologies 61; raw data, limitation 61

learning loss: concerns, distance learning (impact) 5, 16; term, coining 15, 16
learning modalities 25; elements, student identification 82; formative assessments *83*; usage 81–83; variety 82–83
learning process: constructive feedback, negative impact 64–65; direct benefit, absence 66; impact 22; quizzes, usefulness 31
lesson: co-planning, facilitation 76; objectives, articulation 58; presentations, formative assessments (incorporation) 79–80
letter grades, emphasis 94
lifelong learners, development 93
login information, usage 41

mastery: demonstration 30
metacognition, student development 60, 82
misconceptions: formative data points 77; highlighting 84
multiple choice questions, usage 81

observation, value 107
one-question survey, usage 74
online-based formative assessment interfaces, usage 40
online-based formative data (collection), polling programs (usage) 73
on-the-fly formative assessments 74; administration 73; instructional technology, usage 71
on-the-fly formative data, usage 71–74
open-ended short answers, usage 81
organizational formative data analysis, requirements 72–73

peer assessments: collaboration habits/skills, student instruction 89; collaborative learning method 84

peer observations 105–107
peer teams, establishment 118
performance data: analysis, student instruction 93; teacher sharing 97–98
personal learning goals, setting 98
planned formative assessments, instructional technology (usage) 71
polling programs, usage 73
post-pandemic instructional technology, usage 22
practice, usage 106
pre-planned activities, usage 72
principals, data use enabler role 53
procedural knowledge, requirement 61
productive data conversations 59
professional development (PD): administrative team buy-in *109*; co-planning/co-leading 108; program, effectiveness 108; teacher-led professional development 107–109; team, consideration 109
professional learning communities (PLCs) 103–105; usage 105
progress: self-monitoring, data analysis (student instruction) 93; student ownership, increase 61
project-based learning (PBL), activity/interactions (occurrence) 27
prompts: inclusion 13, 80–81; low-rigor prompts, addressing 43–44
public education, instructional technology (usage) 119

questions: development 76; higher-order questions, encouragement 15; inclusion 80–81
quick response (QR) codes, usage 75, 118
quick surveys, usage 74
quizzes: understanding 81; usefulness 31

raw data, limitation 61, 115–116
real-time data, collection/usage (importance) 13
resources (student connection), technology (usage) 64–65
rubrics: comparison *91*; digital self-assessment rubrics 90

scaffolding: data-driven scaffolding/supports, incorporation 28; usage 29
school: collaborative culture *104*; leaders, PLCs (usage) 105; vision, classroom vision (comparison) *115*
self-assessment: component, exclusion/inclusion *91*; personalization 95; rubrics, usage 90–93
self-monitored digital success trackers 90, 97–99, 115
self-monitoring, building 75
self-monitoring skill, importance 99
self-reflection (activities) 98–99
self-regulated learning environments 98
self-selected grouping, usefulness 96–97
self-selected small groups 90, 94–97
shared leadership, culture (fostering) 108
small group instruction 71–72; differentiation 23; informing, understanding 80–81; student identification 55–56
small groups: planning, formative data points (usage) 65; self-selected small groups 94–97
smartphones, usage 31
socioemotional data 110
socioemotional well-being, organizational level analysis factor 42
stakeholders, independent learner philosophy (introduction) *90*
student capacity, building 97; formative data, usage 89

student learning: awareness 58; educator passion 116; modalities, elements (identification) 82; navigation 93; opportunities (differentiation), formative data (usage) 47; ownership 29; re-envisioning 116–119; self-monitoring 98; teacher beliefs/role 26–29; teacher collection/analysis 30
student learning, improvement 12, 15, 64; teaching activities, modification 31
students: academic learning (monitoring), formative data (usage) 44; access, facilitation 46; achievement, gains 7; actionable data understanding 57–62; activation, instructional resources (usage) 29; applications, usage/familiarity 118; at-risk students (success), assessment time (impact) 67; collaboration habits/skills instruction 89; concept/skill understanding, determination 60; cumulative capabilities, establishment 39–40; diagnostic feedback, providing 64; differentiated groups/activities, self-selection 72; differentiation, individualized supports (usage) 46; empathy, usage 60; equitable access, increase 47–48; equity/access, importance 25; experience (focus), vision (usage) 26; expertise, teacher construction 58; formative assessment access process *62*; formative assessment strategies, impact 29; groupings 96; growth mindset (fostering), formative data (usage) 36–39; independent learner preparation 121–122; mastery, improvement 110; mastery, insight 9–10; metacognition, development 60, 82; needs, differentiation 45; performance data, teacher sharing 97–98; performance results 118;

personal learning goals, setting 98; proficiencies, measurement 61; resources connection, technology (usage) 64–65; self-analysis, improvement 97; self-monitoring 62; student-generated formative assessments 83–84; teachers, trust (development) 109; technical expertise, expansion 23; topic exploration, opportunities 30; work, comparison (improvement) 43; work (assessment), rigor (increase) 43

student self-assessment 58; comfort 97

student strengths: areas, self-training 58; information, providing 47; understanding 61

student success: formative data, impact 36; indicators, insight 42; innovation, usage 119; trajectory, change 32

success: celebration events 109–110; criteria, clarifying/sharing 29; self-monitored digital success trackers 97–99, 115; stories, formative data basis 37–38

summative assessment: focus, reflection 120–121; usage 7

summative data: consideration 120–121; loss, impact 5, 13–15

teachers: data use accountability 53; diagnostic feedback, providing 64; feedback 118; input, importance 42; practices, efficacy (evaluation ability) 43; roles, re-envisioning 121; strengths, understanding 61; students, trust (development) 109; teacher-led professional development 107–109; technical expertise, expansion 23

technical expertise, expansion 23

technological resource sharing 108

technology: advancements, impact 5, 6–13; application 24, 108; benefits 31; integration 40–41; resource, limitations 24; usage 64–66, 118

technology-based approach, usage (evaluation) 31

technology-enhanced assessments 6

text accessibility, increase 46

topic exploration, opportunities 30

training: opportunities 109; planning meetings, scheduling 109

virtual peer observations 105–107

visual feedback, creation 98–99

whiteboard, usage 79

whole class instruction: informing 75; on-the-fly formative data, usage 71–74

whole-group review, teacher consideration 96

Zoom, usage 73, 105, 107

For Product Safety Concerns and Information please contact our EU
representative GPSR@taylorandfrancis.com
Taylor & Francis Verlag GmbH, Kaufingerstraße 24, 80331 München, Germany

www.ingramcontent.com/pod-product-compliance
Lightning Source LLC
Chambersburg PA
CBHW061451300426
44114CB00014B/1929